SOCIAL JUSTICE, EQUALITY AND EMPOWERMENT

HUMAN TRAFFICKING

UNITED KINGDOM RESPONSES AND STRATEGY

SOCIAL JUSTICE, EQUALITY AND EMPOWERMENT

Additional books in this series can be found on Nova's website under the Series tab.

Additional e-books in this series can be found on Nova's website under the e-book tab.

SOCIAL JUSTICE, EQUALITY AND EMPOWERMENT

HUMAN TRAFFICKING

UNITED KINGDOM RESPONSES AND STRATEGY

MILDRED SAPIENTI
EDITOR

nova publishers
New York

For permission to use material from this book please contact us:
Telephone 631-231-7269; Fax 631-231-8175
Web Site: http://www.novapublishers.com

Additional color graphics may be available in the e-book version of this book.

Library of Congress Cataloging-in-Publication Data

ISBN: 978-1-63117-675-3

Published by Nova Science Publishers, Inc. † New York

CONTENTS

PREFACE

This book discusses the ways in which the United Kingdom hopes to respond to human trafficking. This includes the draft of the UK's Modern Slavery Bill, and other strategies they hope to use toward ending human trafficking.

Chapter 1 – Human trafficking is a subject of growing concern, both internationally and domestically. There are some difficulties of definition, as various different terms are used inconsistently, and it is also very difficult to get a clear idea of the numbers of people involved in human trafficking. Despite this, there have been various international agreements, studies and campaigns to address the problem. Various legislative and other policies have been put in place, including new trafficking offences and the creation of a UK Human Trafficking Centre.

The Government announced in August 2013 that it would introduce a Modern Slavery Bill, to be published this year in draft form for pre-legislative scrutiny. The bill will consolidate into one act the offences used to prosecute slave drivers, introduce Trafficking Prevention Orders to restrict the activity and movement of convicted traffickers and provide for a new Anti-Slavery Commissioner to hold law enforcement and other organisations to account. The draft Bill was published as part of a white paper on 16 December 2013 and is discussed separately in Library Standard Note 6792 *Draft Modern Slavery Bill.*

This note looks at the UK's responses to human trafficking, including the Government's strategy against trafficking and implementation of the Council of Europe Convention against trafficking and a related Directive.

Chapter 2 – On 16 December 2013 the Government published a White Paper which included a Draft Modern Slavery Bill. The draft Bill contains provisions to:

- Consolidate and simplify existing slavery and trafficking offences;
- Increase the maximum sentences available to life imprisonment;
- Introduce civil orders to restrict the activity of those who pose a risk and those convicted of slavery and trafficking offences;
- Create a new Anti-Slavery Commissioner; and
- Establish a legal duty on specified public authorities to report potential victims of trafficking.
- The draft Bill currently extends to England and Wales only.

Also on 16 December 2013, Frank Field published a report, *Establishing Britain as a world leader in the fight against modern slavery: Report of the Modern Slavery Bill Evidence Review.* He had been asked by the Home Secretary, Theresa May, to lead a series of evidence sessions in the autumn of 2013.

The Home Secretary has said that the Government will

- bring forward a Bill in May 2014, informed by Frank Field's report and the report of a Joint Committee which will conduct pre-legislative scrutiny of the draft Bill.
- publish a Modern Slavery Action Plan in Spring 2014, based on the work produced by Frank Field and others, setting out its non-legislative response to modern slavery.

A Joint Committee to undertake pre-legislative scrutiny will be appointed following motions in both Houses.Further information about human trafficking generally can be found in the Library Standard Note: *Human Trafficking: UK responses* (SN04324).

Chapter 3 – Modern slavery is an appalling crime. It affects victims in ways that are almost incomprehensible. Sadly it is very real and it is happening in towns and cities all over the world. And it is happening here in the UK. Modern Slavery often goes unseen for months and years, it goes unseen in quiet cul-de-sacs and streets and roads around the country.

Victims are held against their will and forced into a life of abuse, servitude and inhumane treatment. We can no longer allow men, women and children of all races, cultures, nationalities and ages to go unseen. We need to take action.

For years modern slavery has been associated with immigration crime. I have sought to change this perception. We will all have seen the news recently that three women had been kept imprisoned for 30 years in horrific conditions. That was in London in the 21st Century. And it has no place in modern Britain.

Victims are frequently trafficked from other countries into the UK, sometimes being deceived into believing that they are heading towards a better life. This is what is known as human trafficking. But what they are heading towards is a life of modern slavery: working long hours for little or no money or food, forced into a life of crime or pushed into the sex industry. Their entire life and liberty is in the hands of another, with no say and no way out.

Chapter 4 – Human trafficking destroys lives and its effects damage communities. The transport and exploitation of vulnerable men, women and children by predatory organised criminal groups is something that no civilised country should tolerate. We need to do more to stop this horrific crime.

The UK has a good record in tackling human trafficking. That is something we must build on. Our new strategy for tackling human trafficking has four key aims: international action to stop trafficking happening in the first place; a stronger border at home to stop victims being brought into the UK; tougher law enforcement action to tackle the criminal gangs that orchestrate the crime; and improved identification and care for the victims of trafficking.

Human trafficking is a truly international crime, with potential victims identified from over 80 different countries to date. We are determined to work more closely with our international partners in transit and source countries to stop this terrible crime. By applying to opt in to the EU Directive on human trafficking, we have demonstrated our commitment to working with other countries in Europe to drive up standards across the continent in tackling trafficking. This is particularly important as we head towards the Olympics and Paralympics in 2012. Monitoring intelligence will help us to respond quickly and appropriately to any potential increased risk of trafficking.

After being taken from a source country and transiting third countries, victims of trafficking must then cross the UK border. For too long our response at the border has not been well enough informed or coordinated. Fulfilling a key pledge in the Programme for Government, in June I announced that we would establish a new National Crime Agency (NCA) containing a dedicated Border Policing Command to strengthen our borders and help prevent human trafficking and other serious crimes.

In: Human Trafficking
Editor: Mildred Sapienti

ISBN: 978-1-63117-675-3

Chapter 1

HUMAN TRAFFICKING: UK RESPONSES*

Sally Lipscombe and Jacqueline Beard

Human trafficking is a subject of growing concern, both internationally and domestically. There are some difficulties of definition, as various different terms are used inconsistently, and it is also very difficult to get a clear idea of the numbers of people involved in human trafficking. Despite this, there have been various international agreements, studies and campaigns to address the problem. Various legislative and other policies have been put in place, including new trafficking offences and the creation of a UK Human Trafficking Centre.

The Government announced in August 2013 that it would introduce a Modern Slavery Bill, to be published this year in draft form for pre-legislative scrutiny. The bill will consolidate into one act the offences used to prosecute slave drivers, introduce Trafficking Prevention Orders to restrict the activity and movement of convicted traffickers and provide for a new Anti-Slavery Commissioner to hold law enforcement and other organisations to account. The draft Bill was published as part of a white paper on 16 December 2013 and is discussed separately in Library Standard Note 6792 *Draft Modern Slavery Bill.*

---

* This is an edited, reformatted and augmented version of House of Commons Library Standard Note SN/HA/4324, published by the House of Commons Library (United Kingdom) January 13, 2014. It contains Parliamentary information licensed under the Open Parliament Licence v1.0.

This note looks at the UK's responses to human trafficking, including the Government's strategy against trafficking and implementation of the Council of Europe Convention against trafficking and a related Directive.

1. Definition

Article 3 of the 2004 *Palermo Protocol to Prevent, Suppress and Punish Trafficking in Persons, Especially Women and Children, supplementing the United Nations Convention against Transnational Organized Crime* set out the following definition of trafficking:

> a) "Trafficking in persons" shall mean the recruitment, transportation, transfer, harbouring or receipt of persons, by means of the threat or use of force or other forms of coercion, of abduction, of fraud, of deception, of the abuse of power or of a position of vulnerability or of the giving or receiving of payments or benefits to achieve the consent of a person having control over another person, for the purpose of exploitation. Exploitation shall include, at a minimum, the exploitation of the prostitution of others or other forms of sexual exploitation, forced labour or services, slavery or practices similar to slavery, servitude or the removal of organs;
> b) The consent of a victim of trafficking in persons to the intended exploitation set forth in subparagraph (a) of this article shall be irrelevant where any of the means set forth in subparagraph (a) have been used;
> c) The recruitment, transportation, transfer, harbouring or receipt of a child for the purpose of exploitation shall be considered "trafficking in persons" even if this does not involve any of the means set forth in subparagraph (a) of this article;
> d) "Child" shall mean any person under eighteen years of age.

This definition has since been adopted in the *Council of Europe's Convention on Action Against Trafficking in Human Beings* and is also cited by the Government in its 2011 publication *Human Trafficking: The Government's Strategy.*

The UK Human Trafficking Centre, part of the Organised Crime Command in the National Crime Agency, gives the following definition:

> Human trafficking is the movement of a person from one place to another into conditions of exploitation, using deception, coercion, the abuse of power or the abuse of someone's vulnerability. It is possible to be a victim of trafficking even if your consent has been given to being moved. Although human trafficking often involves an international cross-border element, it is also possible to be a victim of human trafficking within your own country.
>
> There are three main elements:
>
> - The movement – recruitment, transportation, transfer, harbouring or receipt of people
> - The control – threat, use of force, coercion, abduction, fraud, deception, abuse of power or vulnerability, or the giving of payments or benefits to a person in control of the victim
> - The purpose – exploitation of a person, which includes prostitution and other sexual exploitation, forced labour, slavery or similar practices, and the removal of organs
>
> Children cannot give consent to being moved, therefore the coercion or deception elements do not have to be present.[1]

2. UK STATISTICS

Due to its illegal and hidden nature, there are no robust statistics on the number of people – adults or children – trafficked to or within the UK for the purposes of labour or sexual exploitation. Regarding modern slavery in the UK, in March 2013 the Centre for Social Justice Slavery Working Group said:

> Our research shows that a large proportion of cases are never recognised or reported, and do not appear in any statistics or measures of the size of the problem. There is no consistent grip on the numbers; agencies charged with such responsibility are groping in the dark for a sense of scale.[2]

However, various estimates do exist.

In its Regulatory Impact Assessment for ratification of the *Council of Europe Convention on Action against Trafficking in Human Beings*, published in 2008, the Home Office estimated that there were approximately 4,000 victims of trafficking for sexual exploitation in the UK at any one time.[3]

During 2008 and 2009 the Home Affairs Committee conducted an inquiry into human trafficking in the UK. Its report, published in May 2009, highlighted the lack of accurate statistical information and estimated that there are at least 5,000 trafficking victims in the UK.[4]

In August 2010, the Association of Chief Police Officers (ACPO) published a report that suggested that 17,000 of the estimated 30,000 women involved in off-street prostitution in England and Wales were migrants. Of these women, 2,600 were deemed to have been trafficked and a further 9,200 were deemed vulnerable migrants who might be further victims of trafficking. Most of those trafficked (2,200) were from Asia, primarily China.[5] However, some organisations, for example Amnesty International and the women's charity Eaves, have argued that this figure is an underestimate, possibly due to an "overly prescriptive" definition of trafficking.[6]

Statistics derived from victim referrals to the National Referral Mechanism (see section 5.1 of this note) were set out in *Human Trafficking: the Government's Strategy*:

> ...the UK's human trafficking victim identification and support framework, the National Referral Mechanism (NRM), recorded 1,254 potential victims of trafficking in the UK referred from 1 April 2009 to 31 December 2010, broken down as follows:

Exploitation type	Number of referrals	
	Child	Adult
Sexual Exploitation	99	438
Labour Exploitation	98	267
Domestic Servitude	44	175
Unspecified Exploitation	81	52
Totals	322	932
No of Prosecutions – 2010/11	116*	

* Number of prosecutions recorded by the Crown Prosecution Service[7]

The *Second Report of the Inter-Departmental Ministerial Group on Human Trafficking*, published in October 2013, gave the following summary of the group's assessment of the scale of the problem of human trafficking in the UK:

> In 2012, 1,186 potential victims of human trafficking were referred to the National Referral Mechanism (NRM), a 25% increase on the number of referrals in 2011. Of these, 786 were females and 400 were males; 815 were adults and 371 were children. The source countries for the greatest number of potential victims referred into the NRM were Nigeria, Vietnam, Albania, Romania and China.

Amongst adult referrals, sexual exploitation remained the most common form of abuse identified through the NRM, although reporting of labour trafficking and other forms of criminal exploitation continued to rise. For child victims, both sexual exploitation and forced labour featured prominently. The UK Human Trafficking Centre (UKHTC) Strategic Assessment for 2012 estimated that there are up to 2,255 possible victims of human trafficking in the UK.[8]

3. TRAFFICKING OFFENCES

Until 2003 there were no specific trafficking offences in the UK. Other offences such as facilitation of illegal entry, kidnap, false imprisonment and living off immoral earnings had to be applied instead. However, a number of specific offences have now been introduced. For a review of the operation of current anti-trafficking legislation, please see HM Government, *Report on the Internal Review of Human Trafficking Legislation*, May 2012.

3.1. Trafficking for Sexual Exploitation

On 10 February 2003 a new set of offences of "trafficking in prostitution" came into force.[9] These offences, under section 145 of the *Nationality, Immigration and Asylum Act 2002*, were simply a stop-gap measure, and were soon replaced by broader offences of "trafficking for sexual exploitation" created by sections 57-60 of the *Sexual Offences Act 2003* which came into force on 1 May 2004.[10] The wording of the replacement offences is similar to that in the 2002 Act; they prohibit trafficking into, within or out of the UK for sexual exploitation and attract a maximum sentence of 14 years' imprisonment. Some examples of how the new offences might work were given in the Explanatory Notes to the 2003 Act.[11] These offences do not apply to Scotland, but section 22 of the *Criminal Justice (Scotland) Act 2003* created a similar offence in Scotland of trafficking for the purposes of prostitution.

Unusually, these offences cover not only anything done in the UK by anyone regardless of their nationality, but also anything done outside the UK by a British person or company.[12]

Section 31 of the *UK Borders Act 2007*, which came into force on 31 January 2008,[13] widened the extra-territorial range of the trafficking offences yet further by:

> ...ensuring that facilitating the arrival or entry into the UK of a person for the purposes of exploitation, regardless of where the facilitation took place and irrespective of the nationality of the facilitator, are now caught by the offences.[14]

3.2. Trafficking for Labour or Other Exploitation

Section 4 of the *Asylum and Immigration (Treatment of Claimants, etc.) Act 2004* introduced new offences of trafficking for labour and other exploitation including organ removal or benefit fraud. It is couched in similar terms to the sexual trafficking offences, and covers trafficking to, within or out of the UK for the purposes of forced labour or other exploitation. Like the other trafficking offences it attracts a maximum penalty (on conviction on indictment) of 14 years' imprisonment and/or a fine. Following a Sewel motion debated by the Scottish Parliament on 12 February 2004, the new offence applies in Scotland as well as England, Wales and Northern Ireland.[15] It came into force on 1 December 2004.[16]

Again the offence can be committed outside the UK (by both British and non-British nationals.[17]

This offence remains separate from the offence of trafficking for sexual exploitation in the *Sexual Offences Act 2003*. While there are some minor differences, the two offences are broadly similar (and have identical penalties). The two offences together meet the minimum requirements of Article 3 of the *Palermo Protocol* (referred to in section 1 of this note):

> Exploitation shall include, at a minimum, the exploitation of the prostitution of others or other forms of sexual exploitation, forced labour or services, slavery or practices similar to slavery, servitude or the removal of organs.

3.3. Sex with a Coerced, Deceived or Threatened Person

During 2008 the Home Office conducted a six month review into tackling prostitution. The outcome of the review was published in November 2008; it included a recommendation that paying for sex with someone who is being controlled for someone else's gain (i.e. a pimp or a trafficker) should be criminalised.[18] The then Government took this recommendation forward in the *Policing and Crime Bill*, which had its first reading on 18 December 2008. As introduced, the Bill proposed a new strict liability offence of paying for the sexual services of a prostitute who was being "controlled for gain".[19] There was lengthy debate on the meaning of "controlled for gain", and concerns were expressed that the term could apply in wider circumstances that those the new offence aimed to cover. On Report, a Government amendment replaced the reference to a prostitute being "controlled for gain" with a condition that:

> a third person (C) has used force, deception or threats of a kind likely to induce or encourage B to provide the sexual services for which A has made or promised payment, and C acted for or in the expectation of gain for C or another person (apart from A or B).

During the Bill's Lords committee stage, another government amendment made further changes to the language of the Bill, replacing the reference to the use of "force, deception or threats" with a reference to the use of "exploitative conduct of a kind likely to induce or encourage the prostitute to provide sexual services for which the sex buyer has made or promised payment".[20] The change was intended to ensure that the new offence would cover psychological coercion (for example threatening to report the sex worker to the immigration authorities) as well as physical coercion.

The offence is now set out in section 53A of the *Sexual Offences Act 2003* (as inserted by section 14 of the *Policing and Crime Act 2009*):

> The new section creates a strict liability offence which is committed if someone pays or promises payment for the sexual services of a prostitute who has been subject to exploitative conduct of a kind likely to induce or encourage the provision of sexual services for which the payer has made or promised payment. The person responsible for the exploitative conduct must have been acting for or in the expectation of gain for himself or herself or another person, other than the payer or the prostitute.
>
> Subsection (2) of the new section provides that it does not matter where in the world the sexual services are to be provided. An offence is committed regardless of whether the person paying or promising payment for sexual services knows or ought to know or be aware that the prostitute has been subject to exploitative conduct. In other words the offence is one of strict liability and no mental element is required in respect of the offender's knowledge that the prostitute was forced, threatened, coerced or deceived.[21]

The maximum penalty for this offence is a fine of £1,000. The offence came into force on 1 April 2010.[22]

3.4. Servitude or Forced Labour

During the Lords stages of the Coroners and Justice Bill in 2009, Baroness Young of Hornsey tabled new clauses aimed at criminalising servitude and forced labour.[23] The clauses had been drafted by Liberty and Anti-Slavery International. A legal opinion on the new clauses, issued by the former Director of Public Prosecutions Ken MacDonald QC and Helen Mountfield of Matrix Chambers, said:

> In our view, the existing criminal law offences pertaining to trafficking, the slave trade, false imprisonment and kidnapping are not apt to cover all offences of servitude. In order for the United Kingdom to comply with its obligations under Article 4 ECHR and the ILO, clear, dissuasive and directly applicable statutory criminal offences of forced labour and servitude are needed which penalise and permit effective prosecution of those who subject others to abuse and oppression. Without them, the United Kingdom is vulnerable to successful challenges in the European Court of Human Rights. We are aware of two such challenges in the pipeline.[24]

The then Government's initial position was that the existing criminal law set out adequate protection and penalties in respect of such activities. However, having considered the matter further, it subsequently introduced amendments of its own:

> ...we accept that improvements could be made to the current law through an additional offence in this area. That said, and as the amendments before us make clear, this is a complex subject. This would be an important offence that was subject to serious penalties, and it is important that it should be as clear as circumstances permit. (...)
>
> We think that a slightly different approach is preferable—an approach that seeks to achieve the same aim but that relies for its core substance on Article 4, on the prohibition of slavery and forced labour, of the European Convention on Human Rights. This approach is used for the offence of trafficking for such purposes. Our proposed formulation would follow this approach but without the requirement that the person has been trafficked.[25]

The offences are now set out in section 71 of the *Coroners and Justice Act 2009*, subsection (1) of which provides:

(1) A person (D) commits an offence if—

a) D holds another person in slavery or servitude and the circumstances are such that D knows or ought to know that the person is so held, or
b) D requires another person to perform forced or compulsory labour and the circumstances are such that D knows or ought to know that the person is being required to perform such labour.

The maximum penalty (on conviction on indictment) is 14 years' imprisonment and/or a fine. The offences came into force on 6 April 2010.[26]

4. Convictions and Sentencing

Details of the number of convictions for trafficking offences between 2005 and 2011 were set out in response to a written parliamentary question in July 2012:

Defendants found guilty at all courts for human trafficking offences, England and Wales, 2005-2011 (1)(2)							
Offence	2005	2006	2007	2008	2009	2010	2011
Trafficking for sexual exploitation(3)	12	15	15	24	23	10	8
Trafficking for exploitation(4)	-	6	8	-	2	6	-
Total	12	21	23	24	25	16	8

1) The figures given in the table on court proceedings relate to persons for whom these offences were the principal offences for which they were dealt with. When a defendant has been found guilty of two or more offences it is the offence for which the heaviest penalty is imposed. Where the same disposal is imposed for two or more offences, the offence selected is the offence for which the statutory maximum penalty is the most severe.
2) Every effort is made to ensure that the figures presented are accurate and complete. However, it is important to note that these data have been extracted from large administrative data systems generated by the courts and police forces. As a consequence, care should be taken to ensure data collection processes and their inevitable limitations are taken into account when those data are used.

3) Includes offences under the Sexual Offences Act 2003, Sections 57, 58 and 59.
4) Includes offences under the Asylum and Immigration (Treatment of Claimants) Act 2004, Section 4.

Source: Justice Statistics Analytical Services - Ministry of Justice.[27]

A written answer of 14 January 2009 set out the average sentence for people convicted of trafficking offences:

> **Mr. Grieve:** To ask the Secretary of State for the Home Department what the average sentence was for those convicted of human trafficking offences over the last five years. [243300]
>
> **Jacqui Smith:** The sentences imposed by the courts on those convicted of human trafficking ranges from suspended sentences to 14 years imprisonment.
>
> The average length of sentence however for the offence of human trafficking is 4.69 years although it should be noted in many cases those convicted are serving longer terms of imprisonment as result of convictions for other related offences such as rape, inciting prostitution or immigration related offences.[28]

5. Support for Victims

It is increasingly being realised that anti-trafficking strategy needs to look not only at traffickers but also at the trafficked. Victims of trafficking may be in a vulnerable position and require support and assistance, not least to help them provide information to the police about their traffickers and to prevent them being re-trafficked themselves.

5.1. The National Referral Mechanism

As part of its obligations under the *Council of Europe Convention on Action against Trafficking in Human Beings* (see section 11 of this note), the previous Government introduced a "national referral mechanism" (NRM) to help identify victims of trafficking. Anyone who the relevant authorities have "reasonable grounds" to believe has been trafficked is entitled to a 45 day reflection and recovery period, during which they can access services such as those provided by the Salvation Army (see following section of this note). Details of how the NRM process works are set out on the website of the

National Crime Agency (NCA): see *National Referral Mechanism* [accessed 22 November 2013].

Statistics on the number of victims referred to the authorities via the NRM are also published on the NCA website and the archived Serious and Organised Crime Agency website.

Some organisations have criticised the NRM for the emphasis that it places on a person's immigration status. One report has even gone so far as to describe the NRM as "not fit for purpose".[29] In 2010 the then immigration minister Damian Green said that the Government was committed to identifying and protecting victims and would "look very carefully at the individual criticisms of the system set up in 2009, and act where necessary".[30]

5.2. The Poppy Project and the Salvation Army

On 10 March 2003 the Home Office announced a pilot scheme to provide accommodation for female trafficking victims, which it was hoped would result in the police obtaining more information on the traffickers who brought them to the UK:

> From today, safe accommodation and a range of services will be provided to support female victims of human trafficking through a non-governmental organisation. A six-month pilot scheme located in London will cater for approximately 25 women, on a rolling basis, who meet the criteria for access to the services, including a willingness to come forward and co-operate with the authorities in the combating of international organised crime that could lead to prosecutions of criminals.[31]

This scheme, known as the Poppy Project, currently has 9 bed spaces for female trafficking victims and also provides an outreach service to women who do not need accommodation.[32]

During Operation Pentameter 2 (see section 7.4 of this note) the Poppy Project received £1.3 million of additional government funding to help with capacity building. This resulted in service level agreements being put in place with 17 women's refuges across the country.[33]

On 24 March 2009 the Home Office announced that it would be investing a further £3.7 million over the next two years into the Poppy Project, which would be used for initiatives such as an expansion of supported accommodation and an increase in advocacy workers.[34]

In December 2010, the Ministry of Justice issued a tender for a contract to deliver support services to adult trafficking victims in England and Wales. Providers were invited to bid for funding to

> Deliver effective coordination and monitoring of the provision of support services to secure efficiency and flexibility of service according to demand and victim need and to deliver equal access to support services for all adult victims of human trafficking, regardless of their particular equality and diversity background, or type of exploitation suffered.[35]

In April 2011, the press reported that the contract had been awarded to the Salvation Army.[36] The Salvation Army's website says that its service:

> ...is designed to preserve the dignity of victims, protect and care for them in safe accommodation, and provide access to confidential client-based support services including
>
> - Legal Advice
> - Health Care
> - Counselling
> - Educational Opportunities[37]

The Ministry of Justice and the Salvation Army made the following comments on the contract award:

> Justice minister, Crispin Blunt, said:
>
> 'This funding will allow the Salvation Army to work together with counter trafficking agencies and specialist support organisations to provide an escape route for these men and women.'
>
> Major Anne Read, The Salvation Army's Anti-Human Trafficking Response Coordinator for the UK and the Republic of Ireland, said: 'For many years we have worked with and campaigned for these vulnerable victims, working with government, police and other agencies to help victims of human trafficking.
>
> We are also partners on many of the groups which exist to ensure this issue is kept on the public agenda.'
>
> Mai, a female victim of trafficking from Thailand who has been helped by The Salvation Army's services, said:

'I was forced to work 24/7 as a prostitute and to take drugs - things I didn't want to do.

'The Salvation Army supported me financially, emotionally and physically, getting me the medical attention I required after the trauma I had endured.'

The Salvation Army, which already runs safe housing for victims of trafficking, will use the government funding to provide approximately 25 per cent of support services and commission the remaining support from experienced, specialist groups - ensuring victims get the best available help.[38]

The Poppy Project criticised the decision, saying that it had focused on cost rather than quality of provision.[39] The then justice minister Crispin Blunt said:

> As the Minister who announced the result of the competition this morning, I want to make it clear that although the Salvation Army, which won the contract, will expect to administer directly about 25% of the funds made available by the Ministry of Justice, 75%—£1.5 million a year—will remain available to organisations such as POPPY so that they can provide the services that they have provided in the past. Although the Salvation Army has taken over the leading role, it will not do all the work itself, and we will need to use the expertise of organisations such as POPPY.[40]

The then immigration minister Damian Green said that he hoped the new system of using a prime contractor would help make provision less "London-centric".[41]

Further details of the tender process were provided in response to a parliamentary question in the Lords:

> Asked by Lord Lester of Herne Hill
>
> To ask Her Majesty's Government on what grounds it was decided not to award the contract for support to trafficked women to the Poppy Project.[HL8714]
>
> **The Minister of State, Ministry of Justice (Lord McNally):** The Government's decision follows a rigorous procurement process. A competitive tender was launched in December 2010 and included an open dialogue with six interested organisations. A detailed specification, informed by the dialogue stage of the process, was published in March. Six organisations, including Eaves Housing, which runs the Poppy Project, submitted bids.

> Bids were assessed by a panel comprising officials from the Home Office, the Ministry of Justice, the UK Human Trafficking Centre and the UK Border Agency. The panel considered how bidders had: addressed the tender specification; demonstrated experience of having provided specialist support to vulnerable victims; and demonstrated the capacity to contract with a range of specialist providers, so as to guarantee the provision of support sensitive to the particular needs of individual victims, including gender specific services and services for victims with disabilities or mental health needs.
>
> All unsuccessful bidders received detailed feedback explaining the panel's decision and were given the opportunity to attend debrief sessions. The debrief information is commercially confidential to the unsuccessful bidders.[42]

6. Child Victims

6.1. Support Services

There are no specific support services for child victims of trafficking. They will in some circumstances be supported by local authorities under general provisions of the *Children Act 1989*, which states that local authorities have a duty to safeguard and promote the welfare of children who are in need by providing a range and level of services appropriate to those needs or arranging for their provision by other agencies.

In its 2009 report on human trafficking, the Home Affairs Committee recommended that:

- the Government should carry out a specific nationwide study into the number of possible child trafficking victims going missing from care and how this number could be reduced; and
- each local authority should appoint a specified person to supervise the care of each child, which the Committee considered could lead to better co-ordination and possibly the provision of extra services for those in need of hard-to-access support.[43]

Further details on local authority care for trafficked children were set out in response to a parliamentary question in January 2013:

> **Michael Connarty:** To ask the Secretary of State for Education if he will review the system of placing child victims of trafficking in local authority care. [138422]
>
> **Mr Timpson:** Lone migrant children, including those that may have been trafficked, come into care, and then receive the full range of support and care that all looked after children are entitled to. Local authorities must allocate each child a social worker to assess his or her needs and draw up a care plan which sets out how the authority intends to respond to the full range of the child's needs. This includes ensuring they have the necessary legal and other support they need, including access to health, education and appropriate and safe accommodation, whether through a foster care arrangement, children's home, or supported accommodation. They also have an Independent Reviewing Officer to oversee their care arrangements, as well as access to an advocate and an independent visitor.
>
> Some local authorities are very effective in supporting these vulnerable young people, and others less so. We want all local authorities to come up to the standard of the best. The Government, with support from the Office of the Children's Commissioner, has commissioned a piece of work to examine the practical care arrangements for looked after children who have or may have been trafficked. This will identify good practice as well as issues to be considered.[44]

The commissioned work referred to in the above PQ has now been published: see Refugee Council and the Children's Society, *Still at Risk: A review of support for trafficked children*, September 2013.

In May 2009, the Guardian newspaper published details of a leaked internal report from the UK Border Agency, which suggested that a care home near Heathrow airport was being used by traffickers as a "clearing house" for trafficked children:

> The intelligence report from the Border and Immigration Agency, obtained by the Guardian, shows how a 59-bed local authority block has been used as a clearing house for a trade in children that stretches across four continents.
>
> At least 77 Chinese children have gone missing since March 2006 from the home, operated by the London borough of Hillingdon.
>
> Only four have been found. Two girls returned after a year of exploitation in brothels in the Midlands. One was pregnant while the other had been surgically fitted with a contraceptive device in her arm. Others are coerced with physical threats to work as street-sellers of counterfeit goods. It is thought that many work in cannabis farms.
>
> (...)

> The report, by the immigration agency's national intelligence unit, was passed to the Guardian by a source concerned that too little action was being taken to tackle the problem. It says Chinese children arrive alone on flights to Heathrow before they are picked up by border officials and taken into local authority care. In two thirds of cases, they disappear quickly – most within a week and many within 24 hours. Many flee during fire drills and 10 have jumped out of windows. Others simply walk out of the front door into waiting cars.[45]

In June 2012, the APPG for Runaway and Missing Children and Adults and the APPG for Looked After Children and Care Leavers published their findings from a joint inquiry into children who go missing from care.[46] This drew the following conclusions in relation to trafficked children in local authority care:

> Trafficked children from abroad are particularly being let down and their needs ignored because the authorities view child trafficking as an immigration control issue. Hundreds of them disappear from care every year, many within 48 hours and often before being registered with children's services. The majority of these children are never found again.[47]

The report recommended that the best way to help trafficked children would be to accommodate them in specialist foster care rather than in B&Bs, hostels and supported lodgings.[48] It suggested that a pilot scheme run by Department for Education and Barnardo's to train more foster carers to support trafficked children and/or sexually exploited children should be rolled out nationally.[49]

The report also recommended that a legal advocate with parental responsibility should be appointed for all unaccompanied migrant children, in order to support them through complex welfare, legal, asylum and immigration processes, and to take decisions based on their best interests.[50]

In November 2011, Home Affairs minister Lord Henley made the following comments on calls to introduce a guardian for child trafficking victims:

> ...local authorities have a statutory duty to ensure that they safeguard and promote the welfare of all children, regardless of their immigration status or nationality. We believe that this responsibility should remain with the local authorities, which co-ordinate the

> arrangements for each child to ensure that they are safe and to promote their welfare. Local authorities obviously have comprehensive systems in place to do this. Adding a "guardian" to this framework risks creating yet another level of complexity to these arrangements, which are already strong and ensure the best interests of the child. Even worse, it risks creating confusion for children if plans for their care are not effectively co-ordinated.[51]

The Government's current policy on child trafficking victims is set out in chapter 7 of *Human Trafficking: The Government's Strategy* (2011) and in the practice guidance *Safeguarding children who may have been trafficked* (October 2011).

6.2. Statistics

In 2007 the Home Office commissioned the Child Exploitation Online Protection Centre (CEOP) to analyse the potential number of children who had been trafficked.[52] CEOP's analysis was published in June 2007.[53] It found 330 children fitting the child-trafficking profile, 85% of whom (276 children) were found to be between the ages of 15 and 17. 24 children were found to be between 13 and 14 years of age, and 14 children were documented as 12 and under, the youngest being a 9-month-old baby. Nearly half the children identified were boys, but for most of these boys the type of exploitation involved was not clear. The study cautioned that it should not be used to estimate the total number of children who have been trafficked into and within the UK, but only as a scoping exercise.

In 2009 CEOP published a Strategic Threat Assessment, which built on the work of the 2007 scoping exercise.[54] It identified 324 children as being potential victims of trafficking or exploitation from data supplied covering the 12 month period from 1 March 2007 to 29 February 2008. A grading system was used to show the likelihood that each child was trafficked, with 159 graded at level four (high) and 12 at level five (very high). Victims were identified as originating from a total of 52 separate countries, the most common being China, the UK,[55] Afghanistan, Nigeria, Romania and Vietnam.

Further updates were provided in 2010, CEOP identified 287 children as potentially trafficked in the 12 month period from March 2009 to February 2010, and in 2011, when 202 children were identified as trafficked into and within the UK over the period 1 January 2011 to 15 September 2011.[56]

Since 1 July 2011 CEOP has had lead responsibility for missing children (trafficked or otherwise). Its approach to the problem is set out in its *Scoping Report on Missing and Abducted Children* (2011).

7. Law Enforcement

7.1. Reflex

Reflex was established by the then Government in 2001, in response to the deaths of 58 immigrants in a lorry found at Dover to bring together all the relevant agencies to gather information on organised immigration crime and to plan responses to it:

> We have established Reflex as a multi-agency response to organised immigration crime into the UK, including Northern Ireland. Reflex is led by the National Crime Squad and engages all the key agencies involved in combating organised immigration crime, including police, immigration services, security and intelligence agencies and the Foreign and Commonwealth Office (FCO), in building up intelligence and planning operations against the traffickers.[57]

One of its three key objectives was to target the immigration aspects of people trafficking. It worked with source and transit countries to share intelligence and arrest suspected traffickers:

> At the beginning of 2002 the UK and Romania agreed to establish a central intelligence unit, which was set up in April 2002. During its first year of operational activity 105 criminal groups were identified, 48 were disrupted and 90 individuals were arrested in relation to immigration or trafficking offences. We are rolling out this sort of approach with other countries, including the Czech Republic.[58]

Alongside this development of overseas alliances, the then Home Office Minister Des Browne identified another key component of the Reflex strategy as "the expansion of an international network of Immigration Liaison Officers in countries that are considered to contain key nexus points for transit to the UK".[59]

7.2. Europol

Europol has a Liaison Officers' network to help operational co-operation between the law enforcement authorities of its Member States. It publishes an annual fact sheet on trafficking in the EU, the most recent edition of which highlighted the following potential "emerging and future issues":

- There are indications that use of the Internet increasingly facilitates the transnational marketing of sex workers, in cooperation with specialist web hosts and administrators. It is anticipated that this trend will increase, as will the number of women sexually exploited in less visible, online environments.
- Any further migrant flows from North African and Middle Eastern countries subject to political instability are likely to provide criminal groups with further opportunities for exploitation.
- The practice of trafficking for the commission of welfare benefit fraud is likely to expand because of its large profits (single trafficking groups can generate as much as 125,000 euros per month) and low levels of perceived risk of detection.
- As passenger air fares increase in line with rising oil prices, it is natural that traffickers will reflect this in the cost to victims in terms of transport fees and subsequent exploitation. It may also lead in some cases to a shift towards lower cost overland and sea travel.[60]

7.3. Operation Pentameter

Operation Pentameter was a national joint venture which developed from, and was funded through, the Reflex initiative. It was the first co-ordinated effort to tackle human trafficking on a national scale. Launched on 21 February 2006, Operation Pentameter involved every police force in England, Scotland, Wales, Ireland and the Channel Islands, as well as the United Kingdom Immigration Service, the Serious and Organised Crime Agency, the Crown Prosecution Service and several non-governmental organisations such as the Poppy Project. Its aims included:

- Raising national awareness of the issue of trafficking
- Identifying the scale of the problem

- Improving national and local intelligence about the organised criminal groups involved
- Recovery of victims and reduction of harm
- Asset recovery
- Making the UK a hostile environment for those involved in trafficking for the purposes of sexual exploitation[61]

It had a three-month operational phase which resulted in 84 women being identified as victims of trafficking. A total of 232 people were arrested and 134 were charged with a variety of offences.[62]

7.4. Pentameter 2

Pentameter 2 was launched on 3 October 2007. The Association of Chief Police Officers described it as a "victim focused operation" with the strategic aim of delivering objectives within the UK Action Plan on Tackling Human Trafficking.

> The results of Pentameter 2 were announced on 2 July 2008:
>
> Pentameter 2 results show:
>
> - **167** victims identified
> - **528** criminals arrested
> - **822** premises visited
> - **6,400** police intelligence reports gathered
> - more than **£500,000** worth of cash has been recovered from those criminals arrested and court orders are in place to restrain further criminal assets running into several millions of pounds
> - Of those recovered **13** of the victims were children with the youngest aged just 14 years old.
>
> (...)
>
> Of the 822 premises that were visited, 157 were massage parlours and saunas and 582 residential properties; evidencing the covert nature of the crime. The majority of victims recovered originated from China, SE Asia and Eastern Europe. During the operation 5 victims (three of which were children) who had been trafficked for forced labour were recovered.[63]

The intelligence gathered during Pentameter 2 was fed into UKHTC workstreams (see following section of this note) and was also used to undertake targeted activity with local partnerships and delivery agents including local authorities, crime and disorder reduction partnerships and local criminal justice boards.

8. The United Kingdom Human Trafficking Centre (UKHTC)

Speaking at the closing conference for the Operation Pentameter campaign on 21 June 2006, the then Home Office minister Vernon Coaker announced that the Government would be establishing a dedicated, police-led unit to build on the work of Operation Pentameter in dealing with human trafficking. The new centre, the United Kingdom Human Trafficking Centre (UKHTC), was launched on 3 October 2006 as a multi-agency organisation staffed by (among others) police and officers from Serious and Organised Crime Agency SOCA, the UK Border Agency (UKBA) and the Crown Prosecution Service.

An overview of the UKHTC's role was set out in the Home Affairs Committee's report on Human Trafficking:

> The UKHTC brings together staff and officers from the police, UKBA, Crown Prosecution Service, Serious Organised Crime Agency and social services. According to the Home Office: "The UKHTC provides a central point for the development of expertise and the strategic and operational coordination in respect of all forms of trafficking of human beings....[It] offers law enforcement a 24/7 support line for tactical, immigration, victim and legal advice and has sought to raise awareness amongst police forces about human trafficking in a number of ways". One of the UKHTC's tasks has been to improve knowledge of the scale and nature of human trafficking. In its written evidence to us, the Home Office describes the UKHTC as "the central repository of all data and intelligence on human trafficking." Another function is increasing public awareness of trafficking, in the hope of identifying and rescuing more victims. It recently ran a 'Blue Blindfold' campaign, including posters on public transport and television advertisements, which had the slogan 'Don't close your eyes to human trafficking'. As far as its operational work is concerned, the UKHTC is organised into five core working groups in the areas

of victim care, prevention, research, learning and development and operations and intelligence.[64]

The United Kingdom Human Trafficking Centre is now part of the NCA (which has replaced the Serious Organised Crime Agency):

> The UKHTC is part of the Organised Crime Command in the NCA. It works in a coordinated way within the UK and internationally. Our work to combat human trafficking involves a wide range of partners and stakeholders. We protect the public, target the traffickers and reduce the harm caused by human trafficking.
>
> The UKHTC's partners include police forces, the Home Office and other government departments, the UK Border Force, the Gangmasters Licensing Authority, international agencies, non-governmental organisations (NGOs) and many charitable and voluntary expert groups.[65]

Further information on the law enforcement response to human trafficking is contained in the *Serious and Organised Crime Strategy* published by the Home Office in October 2013.[66]

9. Government Policy

9.1. The Labour Government's Action Plan

In January 2006 the Home Office and Scottish Executive Published *Tackling Human Trafficking – Consultation on Proposals for a UK Action Plan.*[67] They proposed an action plan covering the broad areas of prevention, investigation, law enforcement, prosecution and providing protection and assistance to victims.[68] Responses to the consultation were requested by 5 April 2006, and the Home Office published a summary of responses in June 2006.[69]

Following the consultation period, the *UK Action Plan on Tackling Human Trafficking* was published in March 2007.[70] The then Home Secretary's preface to the March 2007 plan said that it was intended to be a 'living document' which would be updated regularly. In keeping with this approach, revised plans containing updates on each of the main areas of the plan together with a number of new actions were issued in July 2008[71] and again in October 2009.[72]

The plan recognised the need to look beyond trafficking for sexual exploitation to other forms of trafficking such as child trafficking, trafficking for forced labour and trafficking within the UK. Particular areas to address included: making human trafficking part of "core" police business; detecting and identifying victims; providing more support and rights for all adult victims (not just those trafficked for sexual exploitation); and specific measures to safeguard and protect child victims.

Key new measures in the July 2008 update included introducing a 45 day minimum reflection and recovery period for all identified victims of trafficking, implementing temporary residence permits for victims of trafficking for a renewable period of 1 year, setting up a national referral mechanism to identify victims of trafficking, evaluating the results of Pentameter 2 and using the intelligence to undertake targeted activity with local partnerships.

The October 2009 update introduced ten further new measures, with a particular focus on monitoring and evaluating the new national referral mechanism, updating and expanding the online practitioners' toolkit, assessing the scope of labour trafficking and preparing for the possible threat of trafficking around the staging of the 2012 Olympic Games.

9.2. The Current Government's Strategy

On 19 July 2011 the Government published *Human Trafficking: The Government's Strategy*. The then immigration minister Damien Green said:

> Victim care arrangements remain central to the Government's approach to combating trafficking. Adult victim care arrangements will be strengthened, with support offered by a greater range of specialist care providers. This will ensure that victims have access to the care they need, tailored to their particular circumstances and in line with our international commitments. We will also ensure that children remain a focus of our efforts as we look to combat those traffickers who exploit vulnerable children.
>
> A renewed focus on preventing human trafficking is required. The UK is already a world leader in the fight against trafficking but we recognise more can be done with international partners to reduce the threat from overseas. The strategy recognises the importance of working with source and transit countries to target and disrupt the work of traffickers and prevent more vulnerable men, women and children from becoming trafficking victims. A key aspect of our

> approach will be better intelligence gathering and sharing and, from 2013 the National Crime Agency will play a vital role in spearheading our fight against organised criminal groups who are engaged in human trafficking.
>
> The strategy also sets out our aim to better co-ordinate our border and policing law enforcement efforts to prevent traffickers from entering the UK. We will use intelligence to target those convicted or suspected of trafficking at the border as well as developing risk-based indicators to facilitate the systematic targeting of high risk passengers.
>
> We will also ensure we monitor intelligence in relation to key events such as the Olympics and Paralympics to respond quickly and appropriately to any potential increased risk of trafficking.[73]

Key objectives set out in Annex A to the strategy include working with the private sector to strengthen the overall approach to trafficking, working to implement the *EU Directive on Human Trafficking* (see section 11 of this note) by April 2013, raising the quality of decision-making under the NRM, working more closely with other countries and the airline industry, improving UKBA guidance and procedures and (in conjunction with CEOP) tackling the issue of trafficked children who go missing from local authority care.

The Modern Slavery Draft Bill

The Home Secretary, Theresa May, announced in August 2013 that the Government would introduce a Modern Slavery Bill.[74] The draft Bill was published on 16 December 2103 for pre-legislative scrutiny by a joint committee of both Houses. The draft Bill is discussed in detail in Library Standard Note *Draft Modern Slavery Bill.* **NUMBER**

A consultation was launched in October 2013 to feed into the draft bill. A Home Office press release stated:

> Home Secretary Theresa May has asked Frank Field MP, in his role as vice-chair of the Human Trafficking Foundation and as a member of the Advisory Council to the Centre for Social Justice, to lead an urgent public debate about practical and effective ways of ending modern slavery in the UK.[75]

Evidence sessions were hosted by the Centre for Social Justice over the following months, and Frank Field's report was published on 16 December 2013 *Establishing Britain as a world leader in the fight against modern slavery: Report of the Modern Slavery Bill Evidence Review*.

On the same date, written ministerial statements were made in both Houses. In the Commons, the Home Secretary commented:

> The bill will simplify legislation, toughen sentences for slave drivers, and enable the courts to restrict activity where individuals may be at risk. This will mean that more traffickers are pursued, disrupted and brought to justice. The bill will also create an anti-slavery commissioner who will galvanise law enforcement's efforts to tackle modern slavery.[76]

The Home Secretary is planning to introduce the bill, following pre-legislative scrutiny, in May 2014 at the beginning of the last parliamentary session before the planned May 2015 election.

The introduction of a modern slavery act was one of the recommendations included in the Centre for Social Justice Slavery Working Group report in March 2013 *It happens here: Equipping the United Kingdom to fight modern slavery*. The report stated:

> We recommend the passing of a single Modern Slavery Act. This will enable law enforcement agencies to see the law more clearly, and not have to reference immigration law for the appropriate offence if they wish to prosecute for trafficking for non-sexual exploitation. The Modern Slavery Act should also include a mandatory duty to investigate all possible cases of potential modern slavery, and a statement of non-prosecution of victims who had no choice but to commit a criminal offence whilst they were enslaved. The symbolic statement of such an Act would reinforce the UK Government's intention to be at the forefront of the fight against modern slavery, reflecting the serious criminality of trafficking for any form of exploitation and demonstrating that modern slavery will not be tolerated in contemporary British society.[77]

10. The Inter-Departmental Ministerial Group on Human Trafficking

The *EU Directive on preventing and combating trafficking in human beings and protecting its victims* (see following section of this note) requires countries that have signed up to it to put in place a "national rapporteur" to monitor the implementation of anti-trafficking measures and to advise the Government on trafficking issues. In this country, the national rapporteur role is fulfilled by the Inter-Departmental Ministerial Group on Human Trafficking. The group, currently chaired by immigration minister Mark Harper, includes ministers from the Home Office, the Ministry of Justice, the Department for Education, the Department of Health and the Foreign and Commonwealth Office, as well as representatives from the Scottish Government, the Northern Ireland Executive and the Welsh Government. Mr Harper has stated that

> ...the IDMG is best placed to [act as national rapporteur] as it has a unique and strategically important role to play in the fight against human trafficking. It has a remit to oversee and coordinate anti-trafficking efforts across the UK and can effect important and necessary change at the right level.[78]

Some, however, have called for the introduction of a new national rapporteur that is independent of Government. For example, speaking in a Westminster Hall debate on trafficking, Peter Bone, the co-chair of the APPG on Human Trafficking, said:

> Under the EU directive, a national rapporteur is recommended to report independently on the Government's action against human trafficking and be the overarching body for collecting intelligence. In my view, setting up a national rapporteur could reduce the cost within Departments. An independent rapporteur might also be more approachable by non-governmental organisations that might be sceptical of a Government-led organisation, which would lead to greater data sharing and a better picture of the real number of trafficking victims.
>
> Other European countries have appointed a national rapporteur. The rapporteur for the Netherlands is a former judge, and the Finnish rapporteur is a former Member of the Finnish Parliament. They do an excellent job in scrutinising their respective Governments' action against human trafficking, as well as acting as a liaison with NGOs. The problem is that our Government have read the small print in the EU directive saying that countries can have an equivalent to the national rapporteur, which is what the interdepartmental ministerial group is.
>
> The group did not start as a great success. In the first 18 months, it met twice, and two thirds of the Ministers gave their apologies. I know the Minister will say that that has been dealt with, the group has published its annual report and it is doing its best, but I still do not see how a group of Ministers can independently scrutinise what the Government are doing. That is also the view of the all-party

> parliamentary group. Of course, we will wait to see whether the interdepartmental ministerial group is successful, but we have a big question mark over that.[79]

In response, the Home Office junior minister Mark Harper said:

> When I was given the job and told that I was chairing the group, I thought about the arguments for an independent rapporteur and the effectiveness of a group of Ministers. A ministerial group is also effective in ensuring that action is taken, which was my prime reason for being in favour of it. If we want to get things done, whether requiring legislation or otherwise, it is important to have Ministers from across Government working with our colleagues in the other parts of the UK, particularly on an issue that several Members described as one that the Prime Minister takes seriously. If we cannot make things happen, no one in Government can.
>
> I did not understand the criticism from several people about the group not being able to get information from within Government. We are all Ministers in the Government, and if we want to get information from Departments we do not need a statutory basis to do so because we are able to get it. Having thought about it, I genuinely believe that having a group of Ministers is effective in delivering change and making things happen in practice.[80]

The Group published its first annual assessment of human trafficking in the UK in October 2012: see *First annual report of the Inter-Departmental Ministerial Group on Human Trafficking*, Cm 8421. The *Second Report of the Inter-Departmental Ministerial Group on Human Trafficking*, Cm 8731, was published in October 2013.

11. The Council of Europe Convention and the EU Directive

The *Council of Europe Convention on Action against Trafficking in Human Beings* (the Convention) was adopted on 3 May 2005.[81] The full text of the convention and an explanatory report is available on the Council of Europe website. It came into force on 1 February 2008. As at 12 November 2013 the Convention had been signed by 43 countries and ratified by 40.[82]

For a long time it was not clear whether the UK would sign and ratify the Convention, despite having been involved in drafting it. However, following an announcement by the then Prime Minister Tony Blair on 22 January 2007, the Convention was signed on 23 March 2007. On 14 January 2008 the Home Office declared the Government's intention to ratify the Convention by the end of 2008, having made "the necessary legislative and procedural changes". A press notice identified progress already made towards ratification:

> Significant progress has been made towards ratification. This includes the agreement of a provisional implementation plan by the Inter-departmental Ministerial Group on Trafficking in July, the development of models of victim support and the piloting of a victim identification process under the police-led, multi-agency anti-trafficking operation, Pentameter 2. The Home Office also hosted, with the Council of Europe, a conference in London designed to share experience of implementing the Convention.[83]

On 2 July 2008 the Home Office announced that, in order to comply with its forthcoming obligations under the Convention, it would be introducing an automatic 45 day reflection period for victims of trafficking followed in many cases by a further new one year temporary residency permit.[84] The July 2008 update to the *UK Action Plan on Tackling Human Trafficking* indicated that the automatic reflection period and the new temporary residence permit would be implemented by April 2009 and reviewed in April 2010 to assess their impact.[85]

The UK ratified the Convention on 17 December 2008. Announcing the ratification, the then Home Secretary said:

> 'Ratifying this convention helps us build on the existing measures in place in the UK aimed at turning the tables on traffickers and providing victims with protection, support and a voice in the criminal justice system.
>
> 'The ratification is a major milestone in our long term strategy to combat trafficking, as outlined in the UK trafficking action plan. This includes our plans to double funding for the UK Human Trafficking Centre next year to £1.7m.'[86]

The Convention took effect in the UK on 1 April 2009.[87]

In March 2010, the European Commission issued a proposal for a new anti-trafficking directive. The proposed new directive would build on the Convention in the following ways:

What is new in the proposal for a Directive?

The proposal builds upon the 2000 United Nations Protocol on trafficking in persons, especially women and children, and the 2005 Council of Europe Convention on action against trafficking in human beings and brings added value. It follows up on a 2009 Commission proposal which was being negotiated but lapsed with the entry into force of the Lisbon Treaty.

The new Directive covers action on different fronts:

CRIMINAL LAW PROVISIONS, including a common definition of the crime, aggravating circumstances and higher penalties, as well as non-punishment of the victims for unlawful activities such the use of false documents in which they have been involved for being subjected to by traffickers.

PROSECUTION OF OFFENDERS, including extraterritorial jurisdiction (the possibility to prosecute EU nationals for crimes committed in other countries), use of investigative tools typical for organised crime cases such as phone tapping and tracing proceeds of crime.

VICTIMS' RIGHTS IN CRIMINAL PROCEEDINGS, including specific treatment for particularly vulnerable victims aimed at preventing secondary victimisation (no visual contact with the defendant, no questioning on private life, no unnecessary repetition of the testimony, etc.), police protection of victims, legal counselling also aimed to enable victims to claim compensation; special protective measures are envisaged for children such as holding interviews in a friendly environment.

VICTIMS' SUPPORT, including national mechanisms for early identification and assistance to victims, based on cooperation between law enforcement and civil society organisations, providing victims with shelters, medical and psychological assistance, information, interpretation services. A victim shall be treated as such as soon as there is an indication that she/he has been trafficked, and will be provided with assistance before, during and after criminal proceedings.

PREVENTION, including measures aimed at discouraging the demand that fosters trafficking, i.e. employers hiring trafficked persons and clients buying sexual services from victims of trafficking, training for officials likely to come into contact with victims, and of potential victims to warn them about the risks of falling prey to traffickers.

MONITORING, providing for the establishment of National Rapporteurs or equivalent mechanisms, which should be independent bodies, in charge of monitoring the implementation of the measures foreseen by the Framework Decision. Such bodies should have

> further tasks including giving advice and addressing recommendations to governments.[88]

In August 2010, the Government indicated that it would not at that stage be opting in to the proposed directive on the grounds that most of its provisions were already in place in the UK:

> The UK already complies with much of the draft EU directive, which is proceeding through the European parliament.
>
> **No benefits for the UK**
>
> A Home Office spokesperson said: 'While the draft directive will help improve the way other EU states combat trafficking, it will make very little difference to the way the UK tackles the problem as there are no further operational co-operation measures which we will benefit from.
>
> 'Opting in now would also require us to make mandatory the provisions which are currently discretionary in UK law. These steps would reduce the scope for professional discretion and flexibility and might divert already limited resources.
>
> 'The government will review the UK's position once the directive has been agreed, and will continue to work constructively with European partners on matters of mutual interest.
>
> 'By not opting in now but reviewing our position when the directive is agreed, we can choose to benefit from being part of a directive that is helpful, but avoid being bound by measures that are against our interests.'[89]

The Government's "wait and see" position was reiterated by the Prime Minister in September 2010 and by the Foreign Secretary in December 2010.[90]

The final text of the Directive was adopted by the Council of Ministers on 21 March 2011, and was subsequently issued as *Directive 2011/36/EU of the European Parliament and of the Council of 5 April 2011 on preventing and combating trafficking in human beings and protecting its victims, and replacing Council Framework Decision 2002/629/JHA.*

On 22 March 2011, the Government announced that it would (subject to parliamentary scrutiny) be applying to opt in to the Directive. Home Office minister Damian Green said:

> In June, the Government took the decision not to opt in at the outset to the proposal for a directive to combat human trafficking but

> undertook to review the position when there was a finalised text. We have now carefully considered the finalised text. The main risk associated with the text has now been overcome: by waiting to apply to opt in, we have a text that has been finalised and we have avoided being bound by measures that are against the UK's interests.
>
> The new text still does not contain any measures that would significantly change the way the UK fights trafficking. However, the UK has always been a world leader in fighting trafficking and has a strong international reputation in this field. Applying to opt in to the directive would continue to send a powerful message to traffickers that the UK is not a soft touch, and that we are supportive of international efforts to tackle this crime.[91]

The Government indicated that it would implement the Directive's requirements within two years of opting into it.[92]

In April 2011, the European Scrutiny Committee published a report into the Directive that looked at the measures the Government considered it would need to take in order to comply.[93] Damian Green had indicated that primary legislation would be required in order to comply with articles 2 and 10 of the Directive:

- to comply with article 2, the existing offence of trafficking for the purposes of labour or other exploitation under the *Asylum and Immigration (Treatment of Claimants etc) Act 2004* would need to be extended to cover trafficking that takes place entirely within the UK, as well as trafficking into or out of the UK; and
- to comply with article 10(1), the territorial extent of the current trafficking offences set out in the *Sexual Offences Act 2003* and the *Asylum and Immigration (Treatment of Claimants, etc.) Act 2004* would need to be extended to cover trafficking by a UK national where the UK was not the country of arrival, entry, travel or departure.

The Government used the *Protection of Freedoms Bill* to legislate for these changes, and introduced new clauses to this effect during the Bill's Lords Committee Stage. Home Office minister Lord Henley said:

> The first new clause relates to trafficking offences for the purpose of sexual exploitation. Under Sections 57 to 59 of the Sexual Offences Act 2003, it is already an offence to traffic a person into, within or out of the United Kingdom for the purposes of sexual

> exploitation. In the interests of clarity, Amendment 152B proceeds by consolidating these existing trafficking offences into new Section 59A and also adding the necessary additional provisions to ensure extra-territorial application of the offences where a UK national commits a trafficking offence anywhere in the world.
>
> The new clause introduced by Amendment 152C, which relates to trafficking offences for the purpose of labour or other exploitation, follows the same approach as Amendment 152B. In addition, Amendment 152C fulfils another requirement of the directive. At the moment, it is not an offence to traffic someone from Manchester to London, for example, for the purposes of forcing them into slavery, unless the victim has previously been trafficked into the UK. This amendment removes this requirement. This brings labour-trafficking offences into line with sex-trafficking offences, ensures our offences comply with the requirements of the directive and provides better protection against trafficking. The other amendments in this group make consequential amendments to other enactments as well as to the extent clauses and the Long Title.
>
> These provisions will apply to England and Wales only. We have been advised by the Scottish Government that, following the enactment of provisions in the Criminal Justice and Licensing (Scotland) Act 2010, the criminal law in Scotland already satisfies the criminal law requirements of the directive. The Northern Ireland Administration intend to bring forward separate legislation in the Northern Ireland Assembly to achieve a similar effect.
>
> The Government are committed to implementing the rest of the EU directive on human trafficking. These amendments deal with those points of the directive that require primary legislation. The rest we will implement through secondary legislation or by other appropriate means.[94]

The amendments were added to the Bill without division and have since been enacted as sections 109 and 110 of the *Protection of Freedoms Act 2012* (see the related Explanatory Notes for full details). The 2012 Act received Royal Assent on 1 May 2012 and sections 109 and 110 were commenced from 6 April 2013.[95]

During the Lords Committee debate on the new provisions, Lord McColl of Dulwich expressed concern that a number of other legal changes were required above and beyond those that the amendments covered. He therefore asked the minister to outline in more detail the areas where the Government would be introducing secondary legislation and other measures in order to achieve compliance. In the written response from Lord Henley, he indicated that the Government considered secondary legislation might be required in relation to the following matters:

- Article 9 (investigation and prosecution), where we are already compliant in practice to enable access to 'effective investigative tools' but where we may need to transpose into legislation.
- Article 11 (assistance and support for victims), where we already comply in practice through the National Referral Mechanism and victim care model introduced in July 2011 as part of the Government's Human Trafficking Strategy but are considering whether more is required.
- Article 12(4), to ensure that victims of human trafficking are *automatically* eligible for special measures during court proceedings. Under the current regime in the Youth Justice and Criminal Evidence Act 1999, children and victims of sex offences are automatically eligible. Victims of human trafficking who are not children or victims of sex offences are only eligible "if the court is satisfied that the quality of evidence given by the witness is likely to be diminished by reason of fear or distress on the part of the witness in connection with testifying in the proceedings". We are considering whether this is adequate implementation.
- Also on Article 12, in relation to police investigations, we are exploring whether we need to make changes to CPS guidance or introduce Court Rules or secondary legislation to fully implement these obligations.
- Article 15 (protection of child victims etc): Victims are not party to prosecutions, so will not require a representative in this context. Currently, the provision of a supporter (representative) for child witnesses during investigations is already included in best practice guidance but not enshrined in legislation and we may seek to address this.[96]

End Notes

[1] National Crime Agency website, *Human Trafficking* [accessed 22 November 2013].

[2] Centre for Social Justice, *It happens here: Equipping the United Kingdom to fight modern slavery,* March 2013, p16.

[3] Home Office, *Regulatory Impact Assessment of ratification of the Council of Europe Convention on Action against Trafficking in Human Beings*, 6 October 2008.

[4] Home Affairs Committee, *The Trade in Human Beings: Human Trafficking in the UK*, 6 May 2009, HC23-I 2008-09, para 28.

[5] ACPO, *Setting the Record*, August 2010.

[6] "2,600 prostitutes were 'trafficked into UK'", *BBC News website*, 18 August 2010.

[7] HM Government, *Human Trafficking: the Government's Strategy*, 2011, p6.

[8] *Second report of the Inter-Departmental Ministerial Group on Human Trafficking*, Cm 8731, October 2013,p7.

[9] *The Nationality, Immigration and Asylum Act 2002 (Commencement No. 2) Order 2003 , SI 2003/1.*

[10] *Sexual Offences Act 2003 (Commencement) Order 2004, SI 2004/874.*

[11] *Explanatory Notes to the Sexual Offences Act* 2003, paras 104-113.

[12] s60 of the 2003 Act.

[13] *UK Borders Act 2007 (Commencement No.1 and Transitional Provisions) Order 2008, SI 2008/99.*

[14] *Explanatory Notes to the UK Borders Act 2007*, para 101.

[15] Motion S2M-838, Scottish Parliament Official Report 12 Feb 2004 col 5817-28.

[16] SSI 2004/494, art 2 (Scotland) and SI 2004/2999, art 2, Schedule (England, Wales and Northern Ireland).

[17] section 5 of the 2004 Act and section 31 of the *UK Borders Act 2007.*

[18] Home Office, *Tackling the demand for prostitution: a review*, December 2008.

[19] Further details of the proposed offence, and some of the responses to it, are set out in Library Research Papers 09/04 *Policing and Crime Bill* and 09/39 *Policing and Crime Bill: Committee Stage Report.*

[20] See Library Standard Note SN/HA/5219 *Policing and Crime Bill: Lords amendments* for further details.

[21] Explanatory notes to the *Policing and Crime Act 2009*, paras 71 to 72.

[22] *Policing and Crime Act 2009 (Commencement No. 4) Order 2010, SI 2010/507.*

[23] See Library Standard Note SN/HA/5211 *Coroners and Justice Bill: Lords amendments* for further details.

[24] Ken MacDonald QC and Helen Mountfield, Matrix Chambers, *In the matter of Article 4 of the European Convention on Human Rights and whether an offence of servitude or forced labour is required to give effect to it and an amendment to the Coroners and Justice Bill*, 8 July 2009, para 3.

[25] HL Deb 28 October 2009 c1182.

[26] *Coroners and Justice Act 2009 (Commencement No 4, Transitional and Saving Provisions) Order 2010, SI 2010/816.*

[27] HL Deb 25 July 2012 cWA165.

[28] HC Deb 14 Jan 2009 c800W.

[29] The Anti Trafficking Monitoring Group, *Wrong Kind of Victim?*, June 2010, p9. See also Amnesty International press release, *UK: Anti-trafficking measures 'not fit for purpose' and breach international law - new report*, 16 June 2010.

[30] Home Office press release, *Combatting trafficking a key priority*, 16 June 2010.

[31] HC Deb 10 March 2003 c3WS.

[32] Eaves website, *The Poppy Project: Our Services* [accessed 22 November 2013].

[33] HL Deb 25 June 2008 c256-7WA.

[34] HC Deb 24 March 2009 cc11-12WS.

[35] BusinessLink website, *Contracts Finder: view contracts – adult human trafficking* [accessed 18 November 2013].

[36] "Sex trafficking charity loses out to Salvation Army over £6m contract", *Guardian*, 11 April 2011 and "Poppy Project funding redirected to Salvation Army", *Guardian*, 9 May 2011.

[37] Salvation Army website, *Human trafficking victims* [accessed 18 November 2013].

[38] Ministry of Justice news release, *£2m a year for human trafficking victims*, 9 May 2011.

[39] Poppy Project press release, *Government awards trafficking contract to 'prayer and fasting' organisation*, 12 April 2011.

[40] HC Deb 9 May 2011 c982.

[41] HC Deb 9 May 2011 c994.

[42] HL Deb 19 May 2011 ccWA201-2.

[43] Home Affairs Committee, *The Trade in Human Beings: Human Trafficking in the UK*, 6 May 2009, HC23-I 2008-09, paras 153-154.

[44] HC Deb 22 January 2013 c194W.

[45] "Revealed: 77 trafficked Chinese children lost by home", *Guardian*, 5 May 2009. See also "People trafficking: a phone call, a car door opens - and another child vanishes", *Guardian*, 5 May 2009 and "Brown pledges to investigate trafficking of children through Heathrow care home", *Guardian*, 6 May 2009.

[46] APPG for Runaway and Missing Children and Adults and APPG for Looked After Children and Care Leavers, *Report from the joint inquiry into children who go missing from care*, June 2012.

[47] Ibid, p10.

[48] Ibid, pp17-18.

[49] For details of the scheme, please see Barnardo's website, *Fostering: What is Fostering? Types of foster placements – child sexual exploitation and trafficking* [accessed 18 November 2013], HC Deb 23 May 2011 c450W, HC Deb 5 February 2013 cc151-2W and "Sexually exploited children are at further risk in care, says Barnardo's", *Guardian*, 6 June 2012.

[50] APPG for Runaway and Missing Children and Adults and APPG for Looked After Children and Care Leavers, *Report from the joint inquiry into children who go missing from care*, June 2012, p19.

[51] HL Deb 25 November 2011 c1282.

[52] HC Deb 13 July 2006 c2028W.

[53] CEOP, *A scoping project on child trafficking in the UK,* June 2007.

[54] CEOP, *Strategic Threat Assessment: Child Trafficking in the UK*, April 2009.

[55] The internal movement of UK children for sexual and labour exploitation has only recently been labelled as "trafficking"; however, CEOP suggests it has been going on for many years under labels such as "child prostitution" and "grooming for sexual exploitation" (pp36-40 of the Strategic Threat Assessment provide a more detailed overview of internal trafficking).

[56] CEOP, *Strategic Threat Assessment – Child Trafficking in the UK*, 2010 and *Child Trafficking Update*, October 2011.

[57] HC Deb 26 November 2002 c248W.

[58] HL Deb 29 November 2004 c263.

[59] HC Deb 17 November 2004 c1596W.

[60] Europol, *Trafficking in Human Beings in the European Union*, FILE NO: 2565-84, September 2011.

[61] Gloucestershire Constabulary, *Pentameter: operational overview*, July 2006, p1.

[62] Ibid.

[63] ACPO press release, *Major police probe into trafficking leads to 528 arrests*, 2 July 2008.

[64] Home Affairs Committee, *The Trade in Human Beings: Human Trafficking in the UK*, 6 May 2009, HC23-I 2008-09, para 11.

[65] National Crime Agency, UK Human Trafficking Centre [accessed 22 November 2013].

[66] HM Government, *Serious and Organised Crime Strategy*, Cm 8715, October 2013.

[67] Home Office / Scottish Executive, *Tackling Human Trafficking – Consultation on Proposals for a UK Action Plan*, January 2006.

[68] ibid. p3-4.

[69] Home Office / Scottish Executive, *Tackling Human Trafficking – Summary of responses to the Consultation on Proposals for a UK Action Plan*, June 2006.

[70] Home Office/Scottish Executive, *UK action plan on tackling human trafficking*, March 2007.

[71] Home Office/Scottish Executive, *Update to UK action plan on tackling human trafficking*, July 2008 [no longer available online].

[72] Home Office/Scottish Executive, *Update to the UK Action Plan on Tackling Human Trafficking*, October 2009.

[73] HC Deb 19 July 2011 c107WS.

[74] See, for example, "Theresa May pledges modern-day slavery crackdown", *BBC News*, 25 August 2013.

[75] Home Office press release, *Home Secretary begins evidence sessions on modern slavery*, 11 October 2013.

[76] HC Deb 16 December 2013 c82WS.

[77] Centre for Social Justice, *It happens here: Equipping the United Kingdom to fight modern slavery,* March 2013, p13.

[78] Inter-Departmental Ministerial Group on Human Trafficking, *First annual report of the Inter-Departmental Ministerial Group on Human Trafficking*, Cm 8421, October 2012, p1.

[79] HC Deb 20 December 2012 cc311-2WH.

[80] HC Deb 20 December 2012 c348WH.

[81] Council of Europe Treaty Series - No. 197.

[82] The countries that have ratified are Albania, Andorra, Armenia, Austria, Azerbaijan, Belgium, Bosnia & Herzegovina, Bulgaria, Croatia, Cyprus, Denmark, Finland, France, Georgia, Germany, Iceland, Ireland, Italy, Latvia, Lithuania, Luxembourg, Malta, Moldova, Montenegro, Netherlands, Norway, Poland, Portugal, Romania, San Marino, Serbia, Slovakia, Slovenia, Spain, Sweden, Switzerland, the Former Yugoslav Republic of Macedonia, Ukraine and the UK.

[83] Home Office press release, *Home Secretary Moves to Ratify the Council Of Europe Convention Against Trafficking in 2008*, 14 January 2008.

[84] Home Office press release, *Major police probe into trafficking leads to 528 arrests*, 2 July 2008.

[85] Home Office/Scottish Executive, *Update to UK action plan on tackling human trafficking*, July 2008, pp55-56.

[86] Home Office press release, *Government ratifies European convention against human trafficking*, 17 December 2008.

[87] Home Office press release, *UK fight against human trafficking*, 1 April 2009.

[88] Europa press release MEMO/10/108, *Proposal for a Directive on preventing and combating trafficking in human beings and protecting victims, repealing Framework Decision 2002/629/JHA*, 29 March 2010. See European Commission, COM(2010)95 final, 2010/0065 (COD), *Proposal for a Directive of the European Parliament and of the Council on preventing and combating trafficking in human beings, and protecting victims, repealing Framework Decision 2002/629/JHA*, 29 March 2010 for the full text of the proposal.

[89] Home Office press release, *Home Office defends position on human trafficking*, 31 August 2010.

[90] HC Deb 15 September 2010 cc873-874 and HC Deb 14 December 2010 c809.

[91] HC Deb 22 March 2011 c52WS.

[92] HC Deb 29 June 2011 c862W.

[93] European Scrutiny Committee, *24th Report of Session 2010-11*, HC 428-xxii, April 2011, chapter 3. The report was debated in the Commons in May 2011: see HC Deb 9 May 2011 cc977-997.

[94] HL Deb 12 January 2012 ccGC61-2.

[95] *Protection of Freedoms Act 2012 (Commencement No. 5 and Saving and Transitional Provision) Order 2013/470.*

[96] Letter from Lord Henley to Lord McColl of Dulwich re *Protection of Freedoms Bill: Human Trafficking*, 1 February 2012, DEP2012-0194.

In: Human Trafficking
Editor: Mildred Sapienti

ISBN: 978-1-63117-675-3

Chapter 2

DRAFT MODERN SLAVERY BILL*

Jacqueline Beard and Oonagh Gay

On 16 December 2013 the Government published a White Paper which included a Draft Modern Slavery Bill. The draft Bill contains provisions to:

- Consolidate and simplify existing slavery and trafficking offences;
- Increase the maximum sentences available to life imprisonment;
- Introduce civil orders to restrict the activity of those who pose a risk and those convicted of slavery and trafficking offences;
- Create a new Anti-Slavery Commissioner; and
- Establish a legal duty on specified public authorities to report potential victims of trafficking.
- The draft Bill currently extends to England and Wales only.

Also on 16 December 2013, Frank Field published a report, *Establishing Britain as a world leader in the fight against modern slavery: Report of the Modern Slavery Bill Evidence Review*. He had been asked by the Home Secretary, Theresa May, to lead a series of evidence sessions in the autumn of 2013.

---

* This is an edited, reformatted and augmented version of House of Commons Library Standard Note SN/HA/6792, published by the House of Commons Library (United Kingdom) January 13, 2014. It contains Parliamentary information licensed under the Open Parliament Licence v1.0.

The Home Secretary has said that the Government will

- bring forward a Bill in May 2014, informed by Frank Field's report and the report of a Joint Committee which will conduct pre-legislative scrutiny of the draft Bill.
- publish a Modern Slavery Action Plan in Spring 2014, based on the work produced by Frank Field and others, setting out its non-legislative response to modern slavery.

A Joint Committee to undertake pre-legislative scrutiny will be appointed following motions in both Houses.Further information about human trafficking generally can be found in the Library Standard Note: *Human Trafficking: UK responses* (SN04324).

1. Background

1.1. The Current Law

The White Paper notes that modern slavery encompasses human trafficking, slavery forced labour and domestic servitude.[1]

Currently trafficking in England and Wales is an offence under section 59A of the *Sexual Offences Act 2003* or section 4 of the *Asylum and Immigration (Treatment of Claimants, etc). Act 2004.* The offence of forced labour, slavery or servitude is set out in section 72 of the *Coroners and Justice Act 2009.*

The maximum penalty (on conviction on indictment) for each of these offences is 14 years' imprisonment and/or a fine.

Further information about these definitions, offences and about human trafficking generally can be found in the Library Standard Note: *Human Trafficking: UK responses* (SN04324).

1.2. Evidence Sessions and Frank Field's Report

Theresa May announced in August 2013 that the Government would introduce a Modern Slavery Bill.[2] A Home Office press release published in October 2013 stated that Theresa May had asked Frank Field, in his role as vice-chair of the Human Trafficking Foundation and as a member of the

Advisory Council to the Centre for Social Justice, to lead "an urgent public debate about practical and effective ways of ending modern slavery in the UK".[3]

Evidence sessions were hosted by the Centre for Social Justice over the following months, and Frank Field's report was published on 16 December 2013 *Establishing Britain as a world leader in the fight against modern slavery: Report of the Modern Slavery Bill Evidence Review.*

On the same date, written ministerial statements were made in both Houses. In the Commons, the Home Secretary commented:

> The bill will simplify legislation, toughen sentences for slave drivers, and enable the courts to restrict activity where individuals may be at risk.
>
> This will mean that more traffickers are pursued, disrupted and brought to justice. The bill will also create an anti-slavery commissioner who will galvanise law enforcement's efforts to tackle modern slavery.[4]

2. The Draft Modern Slavery Bill

The draft Bill was published within a white paper, with commentary about the wider strategic plan for tackling modern slavery. There are 40 clauses and a schedule. The Bill will be subject to pre-legislative scrutiny.[5] The command paper was published with a Draft Modern Slavery Bill: European Convention on Human Rights memorandum and a Draft Modern Slavery Bill: impact assessment.

The Joint Committee has not yet been established but will begin scrutiny as soon as possible. The Home Secretary's written ministerial statement referred to both Frank Field's Evidence Review and the Joint Committee's report as informing development of the final Bill and an action plan to be published in spring 2014.

Further background on the process of pre-legislative scrutiny is contained in Library Standard Note 5859 *Pre-legislative scrutiny under the Coalition Government.*

3. Provisions of the Draft Bill

3.1. Part 1 - Offences

This part of the Bill would create three new offences relating to human trafficking and slavery, consolidating and changing previous offences. The *Explanatory Notes* to the Draft Bill are drawn upon as the basis for the following commentary.

Clause 1 would provide for an offence of slavery, servitude and forced or compulsory labour. It would replace the existing such offence in section 71 of the *Coroners and Justice Act 2009* which is repealed by clause 10. The wording of the offence has not been amended and continues to criminalise slavery, servitude and forced or compulsory labour. It would also provide for the offence to be interpreted in accordance with Article 4 (slavery and servitude) of the European Convention on Human Rights.

Clause 2 would create a single offence of human trafficking covering sexual and non-sexual exploitation. It would replace the two existing offences in sections 59A of the *Sexual Offences Act 2003* (which relates to human trafficking for the purposes of sexual exploitation), as inserted by section 109 of the *Protection of Freedoms Act 2012* (which replaced the previous offences in sections 57 to 59 of the *Sexual Offences Act 2003*), and section 4 of the *Asylum and Immigration (Treatment of Claimants, etc) Act 2004* (which relates to human trafficking for the purposes of labour or other exploitation); **Clause 3** sets out the meaning of exploitation for the purposes of clause 2.

Clause 4 would create a separate offence under the bill for other offences committed with a view to committing a trafficking offence under clause 2. This separate offence ensures that the preparatory criminal conduct for a lesser offence, for example theft of a vehicle with the intention of using that vehicle to traffick individuals, can attract the higher penalties provided for in clause 5. It is modelled on the existing offence in section 62 of the *Sexual Offences Act 2003.*

Clause 5 sets out the penalties for the offences in clauses 1, 2 and 4.The clause would give each a maximum life sentence, although a court is not obliged to award such a sentence. The *ECHR Memorandum* notes that the offences are included in Schedule 15 of the *Criminal Justice Act 2003,* which means that offenders are eligible for the 2-strikes automatic life sentence in s224A of the Act. The Memorandum notes that the Government have yet to respond to the ECtHR Grand Chamber judgement in *Vinter and others v*

United Kingdom (66069/05) that concerns the Article 3 compatibility of whole life orders under the 2003 Act in the absence of a mechanism for review.[6]

Clauses 7 and 8 deal with the forfeiture and detention of land vehicles, ship or aircraft. The provisions are based on sections 60A and 60B of the *Sexual Offences Act 2003* extended to the new combined trafficking offence in clause 2. The *Sexual Offences Act* provisions were themselves based on provisions in sections 25C and 25D of the *Immigration Act 1971*. The new powers are designed to provide a more bespoke provision for forfeiture. Applications to the court are allowed for release of the forfeited or detained goods.

Clauses 9 and 10 deal with interpretation and repeals.

3.2. Part 2 STPOs and STROs - New Forms of Civil Orders

This part introduces new forms of civil orders to enable prohibitions to be imposed by the courts on individuals convicted of a slavery or trafficking offence, or those involved in slavery or trafficking but who have not been convicted of a slavery or trafficking offence. There are precedents, such as the orders available under the *Sexual Offences Act 2003* or the *Serious Crime Act 2007.* Courts would be able to impose prohibition orders on individuals where there is evidence that the individual is posing a risk of causing another person to be a victim of slavery or trafficking for exploitation. A Slavery and Trafficking Prevention Order (STPO) may last for a fixed period of at least five years and a Slavery and Trafficking Restriction Order (STRO) may last for at least two years. The Draft Modern Slavery Bill: European Convention on Human Rights memorandum acknowledges that Article 8(1) is engaged, but argues that in assessing whether a particular interference with Article 8(1) is proportionate, the Home Office has taken into account relevant EtCHR jurisprudence, including *Stubbings – v- United Kingdom,*[7]

Clause 11 would create Slavery and Trafficking Prevention Orders (STPOs) in detail, providing for the courts to make orders once satisfied that one is necessary and there has been a conviction. **Clause 12** would provide for an application for a STPO to a magistrates' court by a chief officer of police or the Director General of the National Crime Agency, which is currently the lead agency in this area. **Clause 13** defines a relevant offender and **Clause 14** would provide for the nature of prohibitions to be contained in STPOs, as determined by the courts. **Clause 15** would allow STPOs to prohibit a person from travelling to specified country or countries outside the UK, with powers to require surrender of passports. **Clause 16** would enable either a person in respect of whom a STPO has been made or the police to apply to the court which made the order to vary, renew or discharge it. An order may not be discharged within five years of it being made without the consent of the relevant chief officer of police.

Clause 17 would allow for application to the court for interim STPOs, in cases where there is an immediate need to protect a person from harm. **Clause 18** would allow for appeals to the Crown Court and **Clause 19** would make it an offence for a person to do anything prohibited by STPOs or interim STPOs without reasonable excuse. Failure to surrender a passport in respect of a foreign travel prohibition would also be made an offence. Statutory guidance is provided for in **clause 20**, to be provided by the Secretary of State to chief officers and the Director General of the NCA. The guidance would be published but would not be subject to any parliamentary procedure.

Clause 21 would create **Slavery and Trafficking Risk Orders (STROs).** Unlike a STPO, a conviction would not be a condition for obtaining a STRO. There is no requirement for the person in respect of whom the order is sought to have previously been convicted or cautioned in relation to a criminal offence. Application for an STRO is made by complaint. The test for the court in making an order would be that the person in respect of whom the order is sought has acted in a way which makes it necessary to make an order for the purposes of protecting persons generally, or particular persons, from physical or psychological harm caused by the offender committing an offence in Part 1. Orders could be made against adults or persons under 18. **Clause 22** would provide for the nature of prohibitions to be contained in STROs, as determined by the courts and **Clause 23** refers to prohibitions on foreign travel. **Clauses 25 to 28** cover interim STROs, appeals, offences and guidance in provisions similar to those for STPOs.

3.3. Part 3 - Anti-Slavery Commissioner

This part establishes a new statutory commissioner who would encourage good practice in the prevention, detection, investigation and prosecution of offences under Part 1. The Commissioner is to be appointed and removed from office by the Secretary of State and resourced from Government. The Commissioner would not have an independent legal existence as a corporation sole, but would be subject to the *Freedom of Information Act 2000*. The draft

Bill does not provide for a fully independent public official, as called for by some specialist groups (see Part 5 Reaction to the Draft Bill).[8]

Clauses 30 to 34 cover the Commissioner and the functions of the office in more detail. The Commissioner would report on an annual basis based on the annual plan they agree with the Secretary of State. The annual plan and report would be laid before Parliament. The Commissioner could also make a report if they are undertaking a specific programme of work on a particular topic. The Commissioner could make recommendations to public authorities about the exercise of their functions in England and Wales. The Commissioner could undertake research and may support others to do so. The Secretary of State is given power to remove from any report information that they think should not be included on the grounds of national security, individual safety or prejudice a criminal investigation or prosecution. The Commissioner could make recommendations to public authorities and provide information, education or training to any person.

There would be a duty to co-operate with the Commissioner, and information provided to the office would not breach any obligation of confidence. But disclosures of information which would breach the *Data Protection Act 1998* or Part 1 of the *Regulation of Investigatory Powers Act 2000* would not be authorised by the draft Bill. The Commissioner is however restricted from exercising functions in relation to particular individuals or cases. The *Explanatory Notes* estimated that the annual cost of the Commissioner, including staff and activities, would be around £300,000 to £500,000 per annum, based on a calculation of 3 staff from within the Home Office.

3.4. Part 4 – Duty to Notify and Miscellaneous Provisions

This part would impose a duty in **Clause 35** on specified public authorities to notify the National Crime Agency where they have reasonable grounds to suspect that a person may be a victim of human trafficking. Specified public authorities would include police forces and local authorities. This duty would be distinct from the existing non-statutory National Referral Mechanism (NRM) which is a system for children and consenting adults to have their cases assessed. Not all data on trafficking victims in the UK is collated through the NRM. Further information is set out in Library Standard Note Human Trafficking: UK responses (SN04324).

This new duty to report will mean that adult potential victims of trafficking, who do not wish to be referred, assessed and supported through the NRM process will still be referred through for data purposes by specified public authorities. The *Explanatory Notes* estimated that there would be c1500 additional reports from specified public authorities as a result of this clause, with an annual cost of around £37,000 per annum.[9]

Other general provisions include **Clause 39** allowing for commencement and **Clause 38** on territorial extent. The draft Bill extends to England and Wales only at present, but the command paper indicated that the Government were working with the devolved administrations to secure a bill with the broadest UK wide effect. Legislative Consent Motions would be required in the Northern Ireland Assembly and the Scottish Parliament to allow broader coverage.[10] Labour MSP Jenny Marra has begun in September 2013 formal consultation on a proposal for new anti-human trafficking legislation for Scotland. Further details are available from the Scottish Parliament website: Consultation on a proposal for a Bill on human trafficking.

4. The Wider Package Relating to Slavery and Trafficking

The white paper contains a section on the wider package of policies and actions relating to slavery and trafficking. The main themes are:

- Training for police, NHS professionals and employees in the travel industry;
- Strengthening the National Crime Agency's law enforcement response to modern slavery;
- Strengthening border controls to detect victims and their traffickers;
- Guidance on prosecution of victims from the Director of Public Prosecutions;
- Applying asset recovery legislation;
- Preventing exploitation of workforces and supply chains, with an assessment of extending the experience and knowledge of the Gangmasters Licensing Authority;[11]
- Increasing support for victims.

The Frank Field report *Establishing Britain as a world leader in the fight against modern slavery: Report of the Modern Slavery Bill Evidence Review* also covers a broader area than proposed legislation. The report called for:

- Improved protection for the victims of slavery, detailing the protection, entitlements and support that victims are entitled to, and putting these on a statutory basis Crown Prosecution Service guidance on the non-prosecution of victims.
- Examining legislation in California on supply chains, which requires businesses to report on their efforts to eradicate modern slavery.[12]
- Improving the National Referral Mechanism, so that NRM decisions on whether individuals are victims or not, are no longer made by UK Visas and Immigration.
- Reviewing the visa status of overseas domestic workers. In 2012, to prevent possible abuse of the visa system, the Government changed the policy so that overseas domestic workers were no longer able to seek employment with a new employer while in the UK.[13]
- Extending the powers of the Gangmasters Licensing Authority to begin investigations in sectors outside its current remit, such as construction, hospitality and catering.
- A system of guardianship for child victims.
- Compensation for victims by the Criminal Injuries Compensation Scheme.
- Increased policing priority and developing regional forums in multi-agency networks
- An Anti-slavery Commissioner independent from Government and accountable to Parliament, with scrutiny powers over Government policies and power to launch inquiries.
- Appeal or review mechanism for victims to appeal against a negative NRM decision.

The Field report also canvassed a distinct child trafficking and child exploitation offence, stronger sentences, seizure and confiscation of criminal assets, and modern slavery and human trafficking prevention orders for persons who were not UK nationals, to prevent their entry to the UK. The report also called for prosecution of extra-territorial crimes.

5. REACTION TO THE DRAFT BILL

There has been a general welcome for the principle of legislation. The Association of Chief Police Officers said "as the Bill develops, the new legislation will act as a deterrent to those looking to the United Kingdom as a destination for trafficking related activities, and those who choose to commit such abhorrent crimes will be more likely to face prosecution.[14]"

Some specialist organisations have expressed disappointment on the detail. The argument is that the focus should be on victims and on prevention. Caroline Robinson, founder of Focus on Labour Exploitation commented in the *Guardian*:

> ... instead of offering legal clarification, the bill offers confused definitions, a blinkered focus on prosecution and an anti-slavery commissioner whose resources and activities would be controlled by the home secretary. Far from a credible attempt to address a complex problem, the bill in its current form is more concerned with what the UK is seen to be doing than the real impact of our actions. [15]..

There was similar criticism from Anti-Slavery International:

> Director of Anti-Slavery International Aidan McQuade said:
>
> 'We welcome the move to consolidate anti-slavery legislation in one bill; however, the lack of provisions for victim protection in the bill means that not only does it fail the victims of this horrendous crime but also is a missed opportunity for prosecuting the criminals behind it.
>
> 'Currently many trafficked persons are often not identified as victims, especially if their immigration status is irregular when they are more likely to be detained and removed from the country than protected. Many victims are prosecuted, for example those found forced to work on cannabis farms. If the victims are not recognised, then the crime is not recognised and the criminals go unpunished.
>
> 'These deficiencies could be reversed by putting protection measures for victims in the Bill: exclusion of a person's immigration status in considering whether they have been a victim of slavery, provision for a right of appeal against a National Referral Mechanism decision, introduction of a system of guardianship for trafficked children who commonly go missing from authorities' care and ensuring that victims are not prosecuted for crimes they have been compelled to commit while enslaved.

> 'It also disappointing that the Anti-Slavery Commissioner, who will oversee the implementation of the government's anti-slavery policies, will not be politically independent.[16]

Alex Balch, from Liverpool University, argued that the draft Bill did not tackle the root causes:

> ...The draft bill actually draws attention away from the causes of slavery-like conditions in the UK and focuses almost entirely on symptoms – and using the criminal justice system, to catch more individuals who benefit from criminally exploiting others. This is only part of the story – regulation and enforcement of the UK labour market is very weak and patchy, making this a low-risk crime for unscrupulous operators. There is some attempt in the bill to improve the language around victim care but there is little extra resource. This is a complex and expensive area and ultimately requires multi-agency co-operation, which is difficult when many frontline staff have low awareness of the problem.[17]

The children's charity ECPAT UK was concerned about trafficked children's needs:

> While welcoming the Government's commitment to introducing legislation and policy to combat human trafficking and modern slavery, ECPAT UK said that the narrow focus of the Modern Slavery Bill omitted several vital measures to keep trafficked children safe. Notable amongst the omissions in the Bill were a system of legal guardianship for child victims of trafficking, a specific offence of child trafficking to reflect the severity of the crime and a non-criminalisation clause to protect victims forced to commit crimes by their traffickers.[18]

The Children's Society called for the inclusion of guardianship for trafficked children, while welcoming the principle of legislation.[19] The Shadow Home Secretary, Yvette Cooper called for more protection for child victims:

> But Shadow home secretary Yvette Cooper said she would "like to see the Bill go further - particularly to provide stronger legal protection for child victims".

> "It is appalling that two-thirds of children found by the authorities after being held as slaves go missing again because the system to protect them isn't strong enough.[20]

End Notes

[1] Home Office, *Draft Modern Slavery Bill*, Cm 8770, December 2013, p2.

[2] See, for example, "Theresa May pledges modern-day slavery crackdown", *BBC News*, 25 August 2013.

[3] Home Office press release, *Human trafficking: Tough sentences to help end modern slavery*, 18 October 2013.

[4] HC Deb 16 December 2013 c82WS.

[5] Home Office, *Draft Modern Slavery Bill*, Cm 8770, December 2013.

[6] Draft Modern Slavery Bill: European Convention on Human Rights memorandum para 9.

[7] (1996) 23 EHRR 213.

[8] There are international equivalents for the Anti-Slavery Commissioner role, discussed in the Field report at p42.

[9] *Explanatory Notes* Cm 8770 para 104.

[10] The draft Modern Slavery Bill December 2013 Cm 8770 p9.

[11] Further information on the Gangmasters Licensing Authority is in Library Standard Note *Human Trafficking: UK responses* (SN04324).

[12] *California Transparency in Supply Chains Act 2010.*

[13] For background see Library Standard Note *Immigration:Migrant Domestic Workers (*SN04786).

[14] "ACPO welcomes modern slavery bill" 16 December 2013 ACPO Press Release.

[15] "Theresa May's modern slavery bill will fail to provide protection to victims" 20 December 2013 *Guardian.*

[16] "Modern Slavery Bill draft fails the victims of slavery says Anti-Slavery International" 16 December 2013 Antislavery International.

[17] Slavery bill no use without shift in attitudes towards migrants and work 20 December 2013 *The Conversation.*

[18] "Protection needs of child victims overlooked in draft Modern Slavery Bill" 16 December 2013 ECPAT Press Release.

[19] "Children's Society welcomes draft Modern Day Slavery Bill 16 December 2013 Children's Society Press Release.

[20] "The Modern Day Slavery Bill" 16 December 2013 The Labour Party Press Release.

In: Human Trafficking
Editor: Mildred Sapienti

ISBN: 978-1-63117-675-3

Chapter 3

DRAFT MODERN SLAVERY BILL [WHITE PAPER][*]

Secretary of State for the Home Department

HOME SECRETARY FOREWORD

Modern slavery is an appalling crime. It affects victims in ways that are almost incomprehensible. Sadly it is very real and it is happening in towns and cities all over the world. And it is happening here in the UK. Modern Slavery often goes unseen for months and years, it goes unseen in quiet cul-de-sacs and streets and roads around the country.

Victims are held against their will and forced into a life of abuse, servitude and inhumane treatment. We can no longer allow men, women and children of all races, cultures, nationalities and ages to go unseen. We need to take action.

For years modern slavery has been associated with immigration crime. I have sought to change this perception. We will all have seen the news recently that three women had been kept imprisoned for 30 years in horrific conditions. That was in London in the 21st Century. And it has no place in modern Britain.

Victims are frequently trafficked from other countries into the UK, sometimes being deceived into believing that they are heading towards a better

[*] This is an edited, reformatted and augmented version of a White Paper presented to Parliament, dated December 2013. This paper contains public sector information licensed under the Open Government Licence v2.0 (United Kingdom).

life. This is what is known as human trafficking. But what they are heading towards is a life of modern slavery: working long hours for little or no money or food, forced into a life of crime or pushed into the sex industry. Their entire life and liberty is in the hands of another, with no say and no way out.

The nature of this crime is so multi-faceted that it should not be put in one box. Addressing this issue requires tireless and coordinated effort across government, and law enforcement; enhanced cooperation with foreign partners; and increased awareness within communities across the UK.

This Government has already taken steps and sought to understand the enormity of the problem. Yes, there will often be an immigration crime angle but let's be clear; this is organised crime perpetrated by criminal gangs with links all over the world. They have the ability to move money and people without recourse from one end of the globe to the other.

We need law enforcement at every level, from the National Crime Agency to local forces to be engaged in relentlessly pursuing and disrupting these groups. Stopping these organised crime groups at their source will result in more arrests, more prosecutions, but most importantly, more people released from slavery and more prevented from ever entering it in the first place. I want a strong message to go out to any individual or group involved in the enslavement of victims; you will not get away with it, we will catch you and you will go to prison for a very long time.

This Government is committed to tackling modern slavery in all its forms. We are introducing a Modern Slavery Bill. We also need to build our capabilities if we are to make a difference. I have therefore set up a Modern Slavery Unit in the Home Office, and it will be responsible for ensuring that we tackle this problem from every angle, whilst always keeping the plight of victims at the very heart of our policies and in everything we do.

I also asked the Rt Hon Frank Field MP to lead a series of evidence sessions over the autumn. Frank has sought the views of a wide range of individuals in the UK and from overseas who have expertise on this issue. He has produced a far reaching report which will inform both the pre-legislative scrutiny process for the Modern Slavery Bill and our wider, longer term response. I am very grateful to Frank, Baroness Butler-Sloss and a host of others for the work they have put into developing this report and for their dedication to ensuring that modern slavery is no longer a hidden issue. We will continue to reflect on this work over the coming months, as our draft Bill is discussed by the Joint Committee conducting pre-legislative scrutiny.

Of course, only part of this will require legislation. I therefore intend to publish a Modern Slavery Action Plan in the spring, which will set out a comprehensive response to this crime, based on Frank and others' valuable work. We are also reviewing the operation and effectiveness of the National Referral Mechanism, and working closely with law enforcement and the criminal justice system to make sure that we prosecute the evil people involved in this crime whilst protecting the vulnerable victims whose life has been cruelly taken from them.

Today I am publishing a draft Bill. After pre-legislative scrutiny, we will bring forward a Bill for publication in May next year. This Bill will have the benefit of Frank's evidence sessions, and the Joint Committee's scrutiny. If we all work to ensure the provisions within it are as focused and targeted as possible, we will have a Modern Slavery Act in this Parliament.

I am determined to expose this hidden crime; to stop it at source; to bring more perpetrators to justice; and to protect and support victims. I hope you are too.

The Rt Hon Theresa May MP
Home Secretary
December 2013

1. The Threat

Modern slavery encompasses human trafficking, slavery, forced labour and domestic servitude.

It is a global crime. In 2012, the International Labour Organization[1] estimated that there were 21 million victims of forced labour across the world. Victims trapped in servitude, including sexual exploitation, into which they were deceived or coerced and which they cannot leave.

Modern slavery is also complex and varied. Traffickers and slave masters use whatever means they have at their disposal to coerce, deceive and force individuals into a life of abuse, servitude and inhumane treatment. Organised crime groups (OCG) systematically exploit large numbers of individuals by forcing and coercing them into a life of abuse and degradation. But victims are not always forced to come to the UK. Many victims from the European Economic Area (EEA) report that their first contact with a trafficker began with the offer of an apparently legitimate job and so they travelled willingly to the UK, not aware of the horrors that awaited them. Individuals can also be brought to the UK by their own families or family connections often for domestic servitude.

Our current understanding of the exact scale of the problem is limited. The only systematic means we have for collecting data is the National Referral Mechanism (NRM)[2] to which potential victims[3] of modern slavery are referred. 1,186 potential victims of modern slavery were referred in 2012 - a 25 per cent increase on the previous year. Of these, 786 were females and 400 were males; 815 were adults and 371 were children.[4]

Victims may be trafficked within the UK or to the UK from source countries. In the UK, individuals from over 95 countries have been referred to the National Referral Mechanism (NRM). However, ten source countries accounted for 68 per cent of all NRM referrals in 2012. Nigeria was the single largest source with 205 referrals followed by Vietnam (135), Albania (128), Romania (74) and China (55). Among those ten source countries, the UK accounted for 33 referrals in 2012.

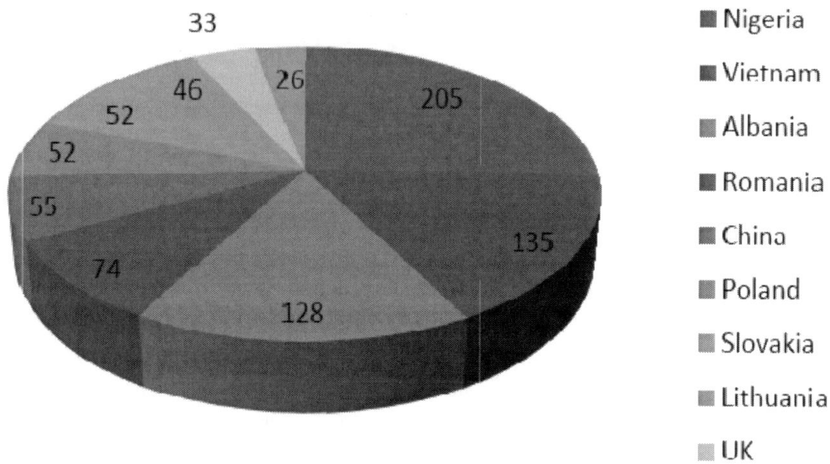

Top ten source countries for 2012 based on referrals t o the NRM.

We know there are more victims in the UK. The UK Human Trafficking Centre (UKHTC) Strategic Assessment for 2012[5] recorded a potential total of 2,255[6] victims of modern slavery in the UK.

And these are just the people we know about.

We believe there are many more unseen and unheard victims. Since 2009, the UK has seen a 48 per cent increase in the number of referrals to the NRM. Increased awareness of modern slavery makes it likely that more victims will be referred in the future.

2. THE STRATEGIC RESPONSE

This Government is committed to tackling modern slavery in all its forms. We need to build our capabilities if we are to make a difference. We must ask the right questions, gather the evidence so we understand the scope of the problem better, and have the right powers and resources available to support victims and bring offenders to justice.

Following the "4P approach" in the Government's Serious and Organised Crime Strategy, we will:

- track down those responsible for modern slavery and bring them to justice, through an improved law enforcement response, supported with better information sharing and intelligence (Pursue);
- stop people becoming involved in the perpetration of modern slavery through effective deterrent measures (Prevent);
- strengthen our protection against modern slavery by raising awareness and increasing our resilience and effectiveness against this crime (Protect); and
- reduce the impact of modern slavery through improved support for victims, both in the UK and those returning home (Prepare).

This will be taken forward in three ways: through legislation in this Parliament; through non-legislative action across the country; and through upstream work in source countries.

The draft Modern Slavery Bill will help to cut this crime and prevent future victims. It will:

- **Consolidate and simplify existing slavery and trafficking offences** to provide clarity and focus when investigating and prosecuting traffickers;
- **Increase the maximum sentence available to life imprisonment** so that offenders receive the punishments they deserve;
- **Introduce civil orders** to restrict the activity of those who pose a risk and those convicted of slavery and trafficking offences, strengthening our ability to cut this criminality;
- Create a **new Anti-Slavery Commissioner** role to galvanise law enforcement's efforts to tackle modern slavery;

- Establish a **legal duty to report potential victims of trafficking** to the National Crime Agency (NCA) to build a clearer picture of the nature of this hidden crime.

Our non-legislative work programme will form the basis of a comprehensive action plan to tackle modern slavery, which we will be publishing in the spring. To inform our work, we invited the Rt Hon Frank Field MP to run a number of evidence sessions to gather information and views from a wide range of experts. His recommendations will be fully considered as we develop the Bill and the action plan.

We must not forget the importance of tackling modern slavery at source, and supporting victims returning home. Our action plan will also set out how we will improve law enforcement action in source countries, and take steps towards scaling up reintegration programmes.

2a. Legislation

The Bill will be the first of its kind in Europe. It will send a strong message, both domestically and internationally, that the UK is determined to put an end to modern slavery. Ensuring that the Bill is targeted and focused will allow it to get onto the statue book in this Parliament. This will then allow future Parliaments to build on the foundations laid by this Government to achieve a slavery-free society.

Pre-legislative scrutiny allows us to test our approach with parliamentarians, frontline agencies and other organisations who see first hand the challenges of tackling modern slavery.

Our immediate legislative priorities for this Parliament are set out in the draft Bill, and we welcome views on these.

Tackling and Punishing the Criminals

Currently, modern slavery offences are littered across a number of different Acts. **Consolidating and simplifying existing offences** into a single Act will make enforcement administratively simpler.

The draft Bill has two substantive modern slavery offences: one for human trafficking and one for forced labour, slavery or servitude. It brings together offences from the following Acts:

- S59A Sexual Offences Act 2003;
- S4 Asylum and Immigration (Treatment of claimants, etc,) Act 2004; and
- S71 Coroners and Justice Act 2009.

The offence of human trafficking has three constituent parts: movement, means and exploitation. The consolidated human trafficking offence reflects these but in a structure, and with language that makes them easier to understand.

The draft Bill also criminalises preparatory conduct: for example, making a visa application with the aim of bringing someone to the UK on a trafficked basis. This builds on the existing provision in section 62 of the Sexual Offences Act.

The **maximum sentence for modern slavery offences** will be increased from 14 years to life imprisonment, ensuring that perpetrators pay for their crimes. The draft Bill will also include modern slavery offences within the extended determinate sentences regime. This means that an individual convicted of a second listed offence will be automatically considered for a life sentence.

These changes will send a very strong signal to the offenders that the UK will not tolerate any form of exploitation and will allow the courts to give stiffer sentences which better reflect the seriousness of these horrific crimes.

Case Study Victim: 'Josef'

A 53-year-old Romanian man named Josef was working as an electrician in Romania. In March 2010, he became unemployed. He met and was given work by another Romanian man.

Josef was badly treated and assaulted from the outset of their working relationship. In October 2010, Josef travelled with his employers to the UK.

He was threatened with violence by them if he did not do as they said. When he got to the UK, Josef was taken to a house and forced to live in the shed in the garden. This shed had no heating or lighting. He was given no food or bedding and was forced to use a hole in the ground as a lavatory.

Josef was then forced to work for the family, stealing and doing work around the house. In March 2011, Josef finally found a chance to go to the police. He was then housed at a safe location outside London.

All four perpetrators were convicted of human trafficking into the UK for exploitation under section 4 of the Asylum and Immigration (Treatment of Claimants) Act 2004 and were sentenced to terms of imprisonment between nine and 13 and a half years.

Restricting Offenders

We will legislate to introduce **Slavery and Trafficking Prevention Orders (STPOs) and Slavery and Trafficking Risk Orders (STROs)**. The nature of modern slavery is so complex that it requires bespoke orders to target effectively the behaviour of individuals and organised criminals operating in this space. STPOs will be available for individuals who have been convicted of modern slavery offences. An STRO can be imposed on an individual who has not been convicted of a modern slavery offence, but only where a court is satisfied that the individual presents a sufficiently serious risk to others. The court will be able to tailor the orders to address the risks posed by the individual in order to protect the community. This could include measures such as being banned from working with children, working as a gang-master or employing staff, or travelling to specific countries.

The draft Bill also includes the power to make interim STPOs and STROs. The interim orders will mean that courts can place temporary restrictions on an individual while the substantive order is considered and made. This incorporates safeguards but ensures that the police are able to act to stop a threat immediately whilst a court considers the longer-term restrictions that are necessary to prevent an individual from committing a modern slavery offence.

Improving Our Response

The draft Bill will also introduce an **Anti-Slavery Commissioner**. Modern slavery damages communities. For the first time, we will have a senior figure dedicated to the UK's fight against modern slavery. The Commissioner will focus on strengthening law enforcement efforts in the UK.

Police and Crime Commissioners (PCCs) have a key role in ensuring a comprehensive local response which fights this crime, and protects and supports victims. They hold their Chief Constable to account for the operational response. The new Commissioner will liaise with PCCs and Chief Constables in respect of the strategic policing requirement in as far as it relates to modern slavery.

The new Commissioner will also work with the Crown Prosecution Service, NCA and other enforcement bodies to challenge the quality of their response and make recommendations on how it could be improved. Appointed by the Home Secretary, the Commissioner will be required to publish an annual report giving an independent assessment on the progress being made to tackle modern slavery.

Improving Our Understanding

A legal **duty to report** all suspected victims of modern slavery will be placed on those public bodies that regularly come into contact with potential victims.

The duty will apply to public bodies identified as "first responders": the police, immigration, and local authorities. Guidance will make clear that victims will be able to remain anonymous if they wish. No one will be obliged to accept support they do not want. Designated non-governmental bodies will also be expected to report all potential victims that they come into contact with, as part of their responsibilities as a first responder. Our approach will ensure that victims can access all the services that are open to them, and that we develop an improved picture of the number of victims of these terrible crimes.

Scope

The draft Bill currently extends to England and Wales only. Recognising that modern slavery is an issue which affects the whole of the UK, we will continue to work with the Devolved Administrations to secure a Bill which has the broadest UK-wide effect.

Northern Ireland

The Minister of Justice in Northern Ireland has signalled his intention to launch a public consultation exercise on the application of these proposals to Northern Ireland. Consultation in Northern Ireland will also consider the most effective means of legislative provision, whether through Northern Ireland legislation (a Bill is currently before the Northern Ireland Assembly) or by extending proposals under this Bill to Northern Ireland, following a Legislative Consent Motion in the Northern Ireland Assembly.

Scotland

The Scottish Government has already made known its intention to explore with the UK Government whether this Bill could be used to legislate for Scottish interests. While modern slavery legislation differs in some respects between jurisdictions, Scotland would wish to retain its current distinctive approach to ensure that the legislative position adopted in Scotland is maintained or enhanced. Any legislative changes covering devolved matters would be subject to a legislative consent motion being approved by the Scottish Parliament.

2b. The Wider Package

Modern slavery is a complex issue that requires a multi-faceted response. The second report of the Inter-Departmental Ministerial Group on human trafficking[7] (the group with responsibility for overseeing and assessing the UK's efforts to tackle modern slavery) demonstrates the complexity of modern slavery and the challenges presented in responding to it.

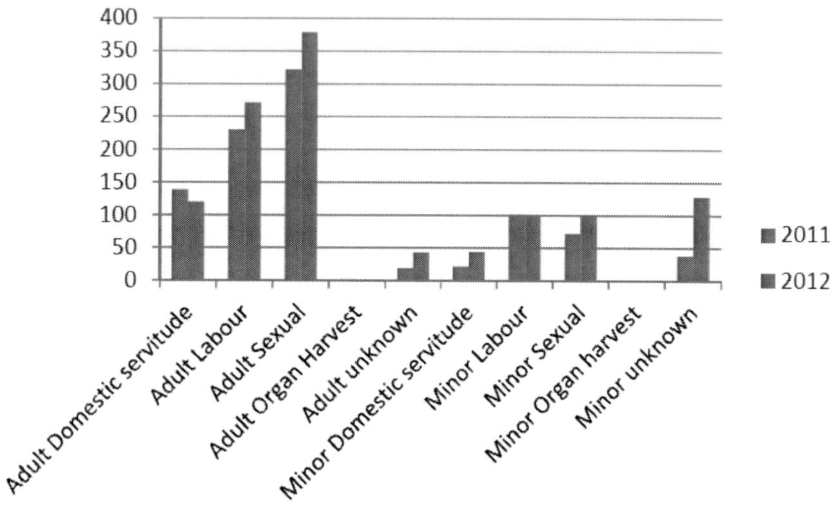

Comparison of referrals by type 2011-2012.

The Modern Slavery Bill is just one element of our strategy, and sets the priority and direction for further activity in the future. The wider non-legislative approach will be fully set out in a Modern Slavery Action Plan in the spring, which will include the following elements.

Raising Awareness and Improving Skills to Respond

To support first responders, the Home Office will provide additional training and guidance to ensure that they fully understand their role, the indicators that an individual may be a victim of slavery, and the referral process.

- The College of Policing will provide training on modern slavery to all front line officers. It will also develop Authorised Professional Practice[8] for those officers in roles that require a more detailed and expert understanding of modern slavery.
- The Department of Health will roll out training to raise awareness of modern slavery among NHS professionals.
- We will continue to work with the travel industry, who play a key role in identifying and reporting suspicious travel activities that may be linked to modern slavery. With the help of Virgin Atlantic and Thomas Cook we have developed a training package for flight attendants who are well placed to spot indicators of modern slavery.

Improving the Law Enforcement Response

We will ensure the National Crime Agency (NCA) strengthens law enforcement's response to modern slavery – internationally and domestically. Under the NCA's new National Control Strategy, modern slavery has been identified as the highest priority level of threat. This sends a clear message to all law enforcement partners.

The NCA will improve international collaboration; and secure increased intelligence sharing with international partners, through Interpol and Europol and following the implementation of new international intelligence sharing systems.

Drawing on new police-developed local profiles for serious and organised crime, we can build an understanding of the threat of modern slavery at a local level and this will inform the work of organised crime partnership boards. These boards include representation from the relevant local authorities and agencies including the police, health and social care and immigration. Regional Organised Crime Units in England and Wales will support the work of local forces by providing specialist capabilities, such as intelligence collection, asset recovery and witness protection programmes.

Strengthening the Border

We will continue to improve our ability to detect both victims and their traffickers at the border. This will include:

- ensuring all frontline border staff are trained on trafficking and child safeguarding so they know what to look out for and what to do;
- ensuring law enforcement agencies share intelligence gathered in-country and overseas, including at the border; and
- better analysis to help officers identify those who may be engaged in or at risk of trafficking.

We will work beyond our borders to encourage other jurisdictions to prioritise anti-trafficking activities and improve returns and reintegration of victims who want to return home.

Prosecution of Victims

We recognise there are concerns regarding the prosecution of victims of modern slavery. The Director of Public Prosecutions will issue revised guidance to ensure that prosecutors understand this issue, and when it is not in the public interest they will not proceed with a case. We will continue to reflect on whether there is anything further that is needed to prevent modern slavery victims being prosecuted where it is clearly not right to do so.

Case Study

Slave Driver: Odosa Usiobaifo

Two girls, aged 14 and 15 at the time, were identified by Border Force officers at Heathrow Airport in September and November 2011 using false passports showing they were adults. They had arrived on flights from Lagos and were attempting to transit to Paris. In interviews with the Serious Organised Crime Agency's Vulnerable Persons Team it became clear that the pair were being trafficked to mainland Europe for the purposes of sexual exploitation. They were placed in local authority care but on 6 April 2012 were reported missing to Sussex Police by their respective foster carers. Investigation revealed that contact had been made with the girls and Odosa Usiobaifo had collected them from a pre-arranged meeting point before they were given false passports and tickets and placed on a flight to Spain.

> One of the girls was refused entry to Spain and returned to the UK. She remains in the care of the UK authorities. The other passed through Spanish border controls and is still missing. It appears that the girls had been subject to JuJu rituals prior to coming to the UK. Usiobaifo was part of an organised crime group trafficking young girls for sexual exploitation.
>
> In March 2013, Usiobaifo was sentenced to the (current) maximum 14 years for his involvement in the trafficking of the girls following a joint Home Office and Sussex Police investigation. He was convicted of conspiring to traffick for the purposes of sexual exploitation and pleaded guilty to conspiring to facilitate illegal immigration.

Asset Recovery

Put simply, serious organised criminals become involved because they believe it is lucrative. We must demonstrate that this crime does not pay.

We will use the Proceeds of Crime Act to recover the money made from modern slavery. Human trafficking is already a "lifestyle offence" under Schedule 2 of the Act, meaning that the courts can confiscate relevant assets linked to a defendant's crimes, whenever those crimes took place, and regardless of whether they have been the subject of criminal proceedings. We will seek to broaden this provision to make forced labour a "lifestyle offence" too.

The general powers of forfeiture in the Powers of the Criminal Courts (Sentencing) Act 2000 will continue to apply to the consolidated offences. We will ensure that the detention and forfeiture powers relating to vehicles, ships and aircraft apply to the offences in the Bill. We will also consider whether we should replicate the approach in the Misuse of Drugs Act 1971 and extend the powers so that they apply to any property that the court deems to have been related to the offence. This would make clear our determination that slave drivers cannot and must not profit from their crimes.

Supply Chains

We will continue to work with businesses on a voluntary basis so they can ensure their workforces and supply chains are not exploited. We will also give further consideration to how the experience and knowledge of the Gangmasters Licensing Authority can be maximised to protect workers in other sectors they do not cover.

Support for Victims

We will continue to support adult victims of modern slavery through the £4 million Government-funded contract with The Salvation Army. We are required to provide victims with 30 days for 'reflection and recovery' but fund an additional 15 days.

We will review the NRM process to ensure that it is the most effective way of identifying and supporting victims.

We will strengthen links between work to tackle modern slavery and our existing programme to tackle violence against women and girls (VAWG). We will carry out a targeted consultation to determine whether the current framework is suited for dealing with those who seek to traffick people into prostitution. We will then take forward actions arising from that consultation.

We will do more to ensure a robust multi-agency approach in response to protect victims who are trafficked or enslaved to provide sexual services.

We will work within Government and with local areas to strengthen support arrangements for child victims of modern slavery. We will ensure robust accountability mechanisms to identify occasions when delivery falls short of the statutory requirements.

We will also ensure that the National Group to Tackle Sexual Violence Against Children and Vulnerable People reflects the needs of victims of modern slavery. The National Group coordinates and implements lessons from recent inquiries into historic sexual abuse to improve cross-Government delivery. This is done by identifying problems and acting swiftly to resolve them.

Case study

Lithuanian farm workers

Lithuanian males responding to adverts placed on the internet and in Lithuanian newspapers were brought to the UK by minibus for employment catching chickens. An agent's fee of £350 was charged to be deducted over time from the workers' pay. A further £120 was charged for travel. The workers were bussed to locations across the UK to catch and crate chickens ready for transportation to slaughter.

They would spend several days at a time in vans, including for sleep. Food was limited and no washing facilities were available. Other accommodation was squalid with shared mattresses on the floors sleeping up to 9 people per room.

Further deductions from wages were made to pay for this accommodation and related heat and power costs. The workers were "kept in line" by a Lithuanian working for the company. Threats, intimidation and violence were used to ensure compliance.

In October 2012, 28 Lithuanian and one Moldovan male were recovered in a police operation and attended a reception centre. All consented to referral to the National Referral Mechanism and moved to Salvation Army accommodation.

3. Draft Modern Slavery Bill

Modern Slavery Bill

CONTENTS

Draft of a Bill
to

Make provision about slavery and human trafficking; to make provision for an Anti-slavery Commissioner; and for connected purposes.

BEIT ENACTED by the Queen's most Excellent Majesty, by and with the advice and consent of the Lords Spiritual and Temporal, and Commons, in this present Parliament assembled, and by the authority of the same, as follows:—

PART 1
OFFENCES
Offences

1. Slavery, servitude and forced or compulsory labour

(1) A person ("P") commits an offence if—

(A) P holds another person in slavery or servitude and the circumstances are such that P knows or ought to know that the person is held in slavery or servitude, or

(B) P requires another person to perform forced or compulsory labour and the circumstances are such that P knows or ought to know that the person is being required to perform forced or compulsory labour.

(2) In subsection (1) the references to holding a person in slavery or servitude or requiring a person to perform forced or compulsory labour are to be construed in accordance with Article 4 of the Human Rights Convention.

2. Human trafficking

(1) A person ("P") commits an offence if P intentionally arranges or facilitates—

(a) the arrival in, or entry into, the United Kingdom or another country of another person ("V"),

(b) the departure of V from the United Kingdom or another country, or

(c) the travel of V within the United Kingdom or another country, with a view to V being exploited.

(2) It is irrelevant whether V consents to the arrival or entry, the departure or the travel.

(3) P's arranging or facilitating is with a view to V being exploited only if—

(a) P intends to exploit V (in any part of the world) after the arrival or entry, after the departure, or during or after the travel, or

(b) P believes that another person is likely to exploit V as mentioned in paragraph (a).

(4) A person who is a UK national commits an offence under this section regardless of—

(a) where the arranging or facilitating takes place, or

(b) which country is the country of arrival, entry, departure or travel.

(5) A person who is not a UK national commits an offence under this section if—

(a) any part of the arranging or facilitating takes place in the United Kingdom, or

(b) the United Kingdom is the country of arrival, entry, departure or travel.

3. Meaning of exploitation

(1) For the purposes of section 2 a person is exploited only if one or more of the following subsections apply in relation to the person.

Slavery, servitude and forced or compulsory labour

(2) The person is the victim of behaviour—

(a) which involves the commission of an offence under section 1, or

(b) which would involve the commission of an offence under that section if it took place in England and Wales.

Sexual exploitation

(3) Something is done to or in respect of the person—

(a) which involves the commission of an offence under—

(i) section 1(1)(a) of the Protection of Children Act 1978 (indecent photographs of children), or

(ii) Part 1 of the Sexual Offences Act 2003 (sexual offences), as it has effect in England and Wales, or

(b) which would involve the commission of such an offence if it were done in England and Wales.

Removal of organs etc.

(4) The person is encouraged, required or expected to do anything—

(a) which involves the commission, by him or her or another person, of an offence under section 32 or 33 of the Human Tissue Act 2004 (prohibition of commercial dealings in organs and restrictions on use of live donors) as it has effect in England and Wales, or

(b) which would involve the commission of such an offence, by him or her or another person, if it were done in England and Wales.

Securing services etc. by force, threats or deception

(5) The person is subjected to force, threats or deception designed to induce him or her—

(a) to provide services of any kind,

(b) to provide another person with benefits of any kind, or

(c) to enable another person to acquire benefits of any kind.

Securing services etc. from children and vulnerable persons

(6) Another person uses or attempts to use the person for a purpose within paragraph (a), (b) or (c) of subsection (5), having chosen him or her for that purpose on the grounds that—

(a) he or she is mentally or physically ill or disabled, is young or has a family relationship with a particular person, and

(b) a person without the illness, disability, youth or family relationship would be likely to refuse to be used for that purpose.

4. Committing offence with intent to commit offence under section 2

A person commits an offence under this section if the person commits any offence with the intention of committing—

(a) an offence under section 2, or

(b) an offence of aiding, abetting, counselling or procuring an offence under that section.

5. Penalties

(1) A person guilty of an offence under section 1 or 2 is liable—

(a) on conviction on indictment, to imprisonment for life;

(b) on summary conviction, to imprisonment for a term not exceeding 12 months or a fine or both.

(2) A person guilty of an offence under section 4 is (unless subsection (3) applies) liable—

(a) on conviction on indictment, to imprisonment for a term not exceeding 10 years;

(b) on summary conviction, to imprisonment for a term not exceeding 12 months or a fine or both.

(3) Where the offence under section 4 is committed by kidnapping or false imprisonment, a person guilty of that offence is liable, on conviction on indictment, to imprisonment for life.

(4) In relation to an offence committed before section 154(1) of the Criminal Justice Act 2003 comes into force, the references in subsections (1)(b) and (2)(b) to 12 months are to be read as references to 6 months.

6. Sentencing

(1) The Criminal Justice Act 2003 is amended as follows.

(2) In Part 1 of Schedule 15 (specified offences for purposes of Chapter 5 of Part 12: sentencing of dangerous offenders), after paragraph 63F insert—

"63G An offence under section 1 of the Modern Slavery Act 2014 (slavery, servitude and forced or compulsory labour).

63H An offence under section 2 of that Act (human trafficking)."

(3) In Part 1 of Schedule 15B (offences listed for purposes of sections 224A, 226A and 246A: life sentences, extended sentences, release on licence of prisoners serving extended sentences), after paragraph 43 insert—

"43A An offence under section 1 of the Modern Slavery Act 2014 (slavery, servitude and forced or compulsory labour).

43B An offence under section 2 of that Act (human trafficking)."

Supplementary

7. Forfeiture of land vehicle, ship or aircraft

(1) This section applies if a person is convicted on indictment of an offence under section 2.

(2) The court may order the forfeiture of a land vehicle used or intended to be used in connection with the offence if the convicted person—

(a) owned the vehicle at the time the offence was committed,

(b) was at that time a director, secretary or manager of a company which owned the vehicle,

(c) was at that time in possession of the vehicle under a hire-purchase agreement,

(d) was at that time a director, secretary or manager of a company which was in possession of the vehicle under a hire-purchase agreement, or

(e) was driving the vehicle in the course of the commission of the offence.

(3) The court may order the forfeiture of a ship or aircraft used or intended to be used in connection with the offence if the convicted person—

(a) owned the ship or aircraft at the time the offence was committed,

(b) was at that time a director, secretary or manager of a company which owned the ship or aircraft,

(c) was at that time in possession of the ship or aircraft under a hire-purchase agreement,

(d) was at that time a director, secretary or manager of a company which was in possession of the ship or aircraft under a hire-purchase agreement,

(e) was at that time a charterer of the ship or aircraft, or

(f) committed the offence while acting as captain of the ship or aircraft.

(4) But where subsection (3)(a) or (b) does not apply to the convicted person, forfeiture of a ship or aircraft may be ordered only if subsection (5) applies or—

(a) in the case of a ship, its gross tonnage is less than 500 tons;

(b) in the case of an aircraft other than a hovercraft, the maximum weight at which it may take off in accordance with its certificate of airworthiness is less than 5,700 kilogrammes.

(5) This subsection applies where a person who, at the time the offence was committed—

(a) owned the ship or aircraft, or

(b) was a director, secretary or manager of a company which owned it, knew or ought to have known of the intention to use it in the course of the commission of an offence under section 2.

(6) Where a person who claims to have an interest in a land vehicle, ship or aircraft applies to a court to make representations about its forfeiture, the court may not order its forfeiture without giving the person an opportunity to make representations.

8. Detention of land vehicle, ship or aircraft

(1) If a person ("P") has been arrested for an offence under section 2, a constable or senior immigration officer may detain a relevant land vehicle, ship or aircraft.

(2) A land vehicle, ship or aircraft is relevant if the constable or officer has reasonable grounds to believe that an order for its forfeiture could be made under section 7 if P were convicted of the offence.

(3) The land vehicle, ship or aircraft may be detained—

(a) until a decision is taken as to whether or not to charge P with the offence,

(b) if P has been charged, until P is acquitted, the charge against P is dismissed or the proceedings are discontinued, or

(c) if P has been charged and convicted, until the court decides whether or not to order forfeiture of the vehicle, ship or aircraft.

(4) A person (other than P) may apply to the court for the release of the land vehicle, ship or aircraft on the grounds that the person—

(a) owns the vehicle, ship or aircraft,

(b) was, immediately before the detention of the vehicle, ship or aircraft, in possession of it under a hire-purchase agreement, or

(c) is a charterer of the ship or aircraft.

(5) The court to which an application is made under subsection (4) may, if satisfactory security or surety is tendered, release the land vehicle, ship or aircraft on condition that it is made available to the court if—

(a) P is convicted, and

(b) an order for its forfeiture is made under section 7.

(6) In this section, "the court" means—

(a) if P has not been charged, or P has been charged but proceedings for the offence have not begun to be heard, a magistrates' court;

(b) if P has been charged and proceedings for the offence have begun to be heard, the court hearing the proceedings.

(7) In this section, "senior immigration officer" means an immigration officer (appointed under the Immigration Act 1971) not below the rank of chief immigration officer.

9. Interpretation of Part 1

(1) In this Part—

"aircraft" includes hovercraft;

"captain" means master (of a ship) or commander (of an aircraft); "country" includes territory or other part of the world;

"the Human Rights Convention" means the Convention for the Protection of Human Rights and Fundamental Freedoms agreed by the Council of Europe at Rome on 4th November 1950;

"land vehicle" means any vehicle other than a ship or aircraft; "ship" includes every description of vessel used in navigation; "UK national" means—

(a) a British citizen,

(b) a person who is a British subject by virtue of Part 4 of the British Nationality Act 1981 and who has a right of abode in the United Kingdom, or

(c) a person who is a British overseas territories citizen by virtue of a connection with Gibraltar.

(2) In sections 7 and 8, a reference to being an owner of a vehicle, ship or aircraft includes a reference to being any of a number of persons who jointly own it.

10. Repeal of existing provisions

(1) In the Sexual Offences Act 2003, omit—

(a) section 59A (trafficking people for sexual exploitation),

(b) section 60 (interpretation of section 59A),

(c) section 60A (forfeiture of land vehicle etc.),

(d) section 60B (detention of land vehicle etc.),

(e) section 60C (interpretation of sections 60A and 60B).

(2) In the Asylum and Immigration (Treatment of Claimants, etc.) Act 2004, omit—

(a) section 4 (trafficking people for exploitation),

(b) section 5(3) and (4) (section 4 - supplementary provision).

(3) In the Coroners and Justice Act 2009, omit section 71 (slavery, servitude and forced or compulsory labour).

PART 2
PREVENTION ORDERS
Slavery and trafficking prevention orders

11. Slavery and trafficking prevention orders on sentencing

(1) A court may make an order under this section against a person ("the defendant") where it deals with the defendant in respect of—

(a) a conviction for a slavery or human trafficking offence,

(b) a finding that the defendant is not guilty of a slavery or human trafficking offence by reason of insanity, or

(c) a finding that the defendant is under a disability and has done the act charged against the defendant in respect of a slavery or human trafficking offence.

(2) The court may make the order only if it is satisfied that it is necessary to do so for the purpose of protecting persons generally, or particular persons, from physical or psychological harm caused by the defendant committing an offence under Part 1.

(3) A "slavery or human trafficking offence" means an offence listed in the Schedule.

(4) For the purposes of this section, convictions and findings include those taking place before this section comes into force.

12. Slavery and trafficking prevention orders on application

(1) A magistrates' court may make an order under this section against a person ("the defendant") on an application by—

(a) a chief officer of police, or

(b) the Director General of the National Crime Agency ("the Director General").

(2) The court may make the order only if it is satisfied that—

(a) the defendant is a relevant offender (see section 13), and

(b) since the defendant first became a relevant offender, the defendant has acted in a way which makes it necessary to make the order for the purpose of protecting persons generally, or particular persons, from physical or psychological harm caused by the defendant committing an offence under Part 1.

(3) A chief officer of police may make an application under this section only in respect of a person—

(a) who lives in the chief officer's police area, or

(b) who the chief officer believes is in that area or is intending to come to it.

(4) The Director General must give notice of any application the Director General makes under this section to the chief officer of police for—

(a) the police area where the person in question lives, or

(b) a police area which the Director General believes the person is in or is intending to come to.

(5) An application under this section is to be made by complaint.

(6) The acts of the defendant which may be relied on for the purposes of subsection (2)(b) include acts taking place before this section comes into force.

13 Meaning of "relevant offender"

(1) A person is a "relevant offender" for the purposes of section 12 if subsection (2) or (3) applies to the person.

(2) This subsection applies to a person if—

(a) the person has been convicted of a slavery or human trafficking offence,

(b) a court has made a finding that the person is not guilty of a slavery or human trafficking offence by reason of insanity,

(c) a court has made a finding that the person is under a disability and has done the act charged against the person in respect of a slavery or human trafficking offence, or

(d) the person has been cautioned in respect of a slavery or human trafficking offence.

(3) This subsection applies to a person if, under the law of a country outside the United Kingdom—

(a) the person has been convicted of an equivalent offence (whether or not the person has been punished for it),

(b) a court has made, in relation to an equivalent offence, a finding equivalent to a finding that the person is not guilty by reason of insanity,

(c) a court has made, in relation to an equivalent offence, a finding equivalent to a finding that the person is under a disability and has done the act charged against the person, or

(d) the person has been cautioned in respect of an equivalent offence.

(4) An "equivalent offence" means an act which—

(a) constituted an offence under the law of the country concerned, and

(b) would have constituted a slavery or human trafficking offence under the law of England and Wales if it had been done in England and Wales, or by a UK national, or as regards the United Kingdom.

(5) For the purposes of subsection (4) an act punishable under the law of a country outside the United Kingdom constitutes an offence under that law, however it is described in that law.

(6) On an application under section 12 where subsection (3) is alleged to apply to the defendant, the condition in subsection (4)(b) is to be taken as met unless— (a) not later than provided by rules of court, the defendant serves on the applicant a notice which states that in the defendant's opinion the condition is not met, shows the grounds for that opinion, and requires the applicant to prove that the condition is met, or

(b) the court permits the defendant to require the applicant to prove that the condition is met without service of such a notice.

(7) References in this section to convictions, findings and cautions include those taking place before this section comes into force.

14. Effect of slavery and trafficking prevention orders

(1) An order under section 11 or 12 (a "slavery and trafficking prevention order") prohibits the defendant from doing anything described in the order.

(2) The only prohibitions that may be included in the order are those which the court is satisfied are necessary for the purpose of protecting persons

generally, or particular persons, from physical or psychological harm caused by the defendant committing an offence under Part 1.

(3) Subject to section 15(1), a prohibition contained in a slavery and trafficking prevention order has effect—

(a) for a fixed period, specified in the order, of at least 5 years, or

(b) until further order.

(4) A slavery and trafficking prevention order—

(a) may specify that some of its prohibitions have effect until further order and some for a fixed period;

(b) may specify different periods for different prohibitions.

(5) If a court makes a slavery and trafficking prevention order in relation to a person who is already subject to such an order (whether made by that court or another), the earlier order ceases to have effect.

15. Prohibitions on foreign travel

(1) A prohibition on foreign travel contained in a slavery and trafficking prevention order must be for a fixed period of not more than 5 years.

(2) A "prohibition on foreign travel" means—

(a) a prohibition on travelling to any country outside the United Kingdom named or described in the order,

(b) a prohibition on travelling to any country outside the United Kingdom other than a country named or described in the order, or

(c) a prohibition on travelling to any country outside the United Kingdom.

(3) Subsection (1) does not prevent a prohibition on foreign travel from being extended for a further period (of no more than 5 years each time) under section 16.

(4) A slavery and trafficking prevention order that contains a prohibition within subsection (2)(c) must require the defendant to surrender all of the defendant's passports at a police station specified in the order—

(a) on or before the date when the prohibition takes effect, or

(b) within a period specified in the order.

(5) Any passports surrendered must be returned as soon as reasonably practicable after the person ceases to be subject to a slavery and trafficking prevention order containing a prohibition within subsection (2)(c).

(6) Subsection (5) does not apply in relation to—

(a) a passport issued by or on behalf of the authorities of a country outside the United Kingdom if the passport has been returned to those authorities;

(b) a passport issued by or on behalf of an international organisation if the passport has been returned to that organisation.

16. Variation, renewal and discharge

(1) A person within subsection (2) may apply to the appropriate court for an order varying, renewing or discharging a slavery and trafficking prevention order.

(2) The persons are—

(a) the defendant;

(b) the chief officer of police for the area in which the defendant lives;

(c) a chief officer of police who believes that the defendant is in, or is intending to come to, that officer's police area;

(d) where the order was made on an application by a chief officer of police under section 12, that officer.

(3) An application under subsection (1) may be made—

(a) where the appropriate court is the Crown Court, in accordance with rules of court;

(b) in any other case, by complaint.

(4) On the application the court, after hearing—

(a) the person making the application, and

(b) the other persons mentioned in subsection (2) (if they wish to be heard), may make any order varying, renewing or discharging the slavery and trafficking prevention order that the court considers appropriate.

(5) An order may be renewed, or varied so as to impose additional prohibitions on the defendant, only if the court is satisfied that it is necessary to do so for the purpose of protecting persons generally, or particular persons, from physical or psychological harm caused by the defendant committing an offence under Part 1.

(6) Any renewed or varied order may contain only those prohibitions which the court is satisfied are necessary for that purpose.

(7) The court must not discharge an order before the end of 5 years beginning with the day on which the order was made, without the consent of the defendant and—

(a) where the application is made by the defendant, the chief officer of police for the area in which the defendant lives;

(b) where the application is made by a chief officer of police, that chief officer.

(8) Subsection (7) does not apply to an order containing a prohibition on foreign travel and no other prohibitions.

(9) In this section "the appropriate court" means—

(a) where the Crown Court or the Court of Appeal made the slavery and trafficking prevention order, the Crown Court;

(b) where a magistrates' court made the order, a magistrates' court;

(c) where a youth court made the order, a youth court.

17. Interim slavery and trafficking prevention orders

(1) This section applies where an application under section 12 ("the main application") has not been determined.

(2) An application for an order under this section (an "interim slavery and trafficking prevention order")—

(a) may be made by the complaint by which the main application is made, or

(b) if the main application has been made, may be made by the person who has made that application, by complaint to the court to which that application has been made.

(3) The court may, if it considers it just to do so, make an interim slavery and trafficking prevention order, prohibiting the defendant from doing anything described in the order.

(4) Such an order—

(a) has effect only for a fixed period, specified in the order;

(b) ceases to have effect, if it has not already done so, on the determination of the main application.

(5) The applicant or the defendant may by complaint apply to the court that made the interim slavery and trafficking prevention order for the order to be varied, renewed or discharged.

18. Appeals

(1) A defendant may appeal against the making of a slavery and trafficking prevention order—

(a) where the order was made under section 11(1)(a), as if the order were a sentence passed on the defendant for the offence;

(b) where the order was made under section 11(1)(b) or (c), as if the defendant had been convicted of the offence and the order were a sentence passed on the defendant for that offence;

(c) where the order was made on an application under section 12, to the Crown Court.

(2) A defendant may appeal to the Crown Court against the making of an interim slavery and trafficking prevention order.

(3) A defendant may appeal against the making of an order under section 16, or the refusal to make such an order—

(a) where the application for such an order was made to the Crown Court, to the Court of Appeal;

(b) in any other case, to the Crown Court.

(4) On an appeal under subsection (1)(c), (2) or (3)(b), the Crown Court may make such orders as may be necessary to give effect to its determination of the appeal, and may also make such incidental or consequential orders as appear to it to be just.

(5) Any order made by the Crown Court on an appeal under subsection (1)(c) or (2) is for the purposes of section 16(9) or 17(5) (respectively) to be treated as if it were an order of the court from which the appeal was brought.

(6) Subsection (5) does not apply to an order directing that an application be re- heard by a magistrates' court.

19. Offences

(1) A person who, without reasonable excuse, does anything that the person is prohibited from doing by—

(a) a slavery and trafficking prevention order, or

(b) an interim slavery and trafficking prevention order, commits an offence.

(2) A person commits an offence if, without reasonable excuse, the person fails to comply with a requirement imposed under section 15(4).

(3) A person guilty of an offence under this section is liable—

(a) on conviction on indictment, to imprisonment for a term not exceeding 5 years;

(b) on summary conviction, to imprisonment for a term not exceeding 6 months or a fine not exceeding £5,000 or both.

(4) Where a person is convicted of an offence under this section, it is not open to the court by or before which the person is convicted to make an order for conditional discharge in respect of the offence.

20. Guidance

(1) The Secretary of State must issue guidance to chief officers of police and to the Director General of the National Crime Agency in relation to the exercise by them of their powers with regard to slavery and trafficking prevention orders and interim slavery and trafficking prevention orders.

(2) The Secretary of State may, from time to time, revise the guidance issued under subsection (1).

(3) The Secretary of State must arrange for any guidance issued or revised under this section to be published in a way the Secretary of State considers appropriate.

Slavery and trafficking risk orders

21. Slavery and trafficking risk orders

(1) A magistrates' court may make an order under this section against a person ("the defendant") on an application by—

(a) a chief officer of police, or

(b) the Director General of the National Crime Agency ("the Director General").

(2) The court may make the order only if it is satisfied that the defendant has acted in a way which makes it necessary to make the order for the purpose of protecting persons generally, or particular persons, from physical or psychological harm caused by the defendant committing an offence under Part 1.

(3) A chief officer of police may make an application under this section only in respect of a person—

(a) who lives in the chief officer's police area, or

(b) who the chief officer believes is in that area or is intending to come to it.

(4) The Director General must give notice of any application the Director General makes under this section to the chief officer of police for—

(a) the police area where the person in question lives, or

(b) a police area which the Director General believes the person is in or is intending to come to.

(5) An application under this section is to be made by complaint.

(6) The acts of the defendant which may be relied on for the purposes of subsection (2) include acts taking place before this section comes into force.

22. Effect of slavery and trafficking risk orders

(1) An order under section 21 (a "slavery and trafficking risk order") prohibits the defendant from doing anything described in the order.

(2) The only prohibitions that may be included in the order are those which the court is satisfied are necessary for the purpose of protecting persons generally, or particular persons, from physical or psychological harm caused by the defendant committing an offence under Part 1.

(3) Subject to section 23(1), a prohibition contained in a slavery and trafficking risk order has effect—

(a) for a fixed period, specified in the order, of at least 2 years, or

(b) until further order.

(4) A slavery and trafficking risk order—

(a) may specify that some of its prohibitions have effect until further order and some for a fixed period;

(b) may specify different periods for different prohibitions.

(5) Where a court makes a slavery and trafficking risk order in relation to a person who is already subject to such an order (whether made by that court or another), the earlier order ceases to have effect.

23. Prohibitions on foreign travel

(1) A prohibition on foreign travel contained in a slavery and trafficking risk order must be for a fixed period of not more than 5 years.

(2) A "prohibition on foreign travel" means—

(a) a prohibition on travelling to any country outside the United Kingdom named or described in the order,

(b) a prohibition on travelling to any country outside the United Kingdom other than a country named or described in the order, or

(c) a prohibition on travelling to any country outside the United Kingdom.

(3) Subsection (1) does not prevent a prohibition on foreign travel from being extended for a further period (of no more than 5 years each time) under section 24.

(4) A slavery and trafficking risk order that contains a prohibition within subsection (2)(c) must require the defendant to surrender all of the defendant's passports at a police station specified in the order—

(a) on or before the date when the prohibition takes effect, or

(b) within a period specified in the order.

(5) Any passports surrendered must be returned as soon as reasonably practicable after the person ceases to be subject to a slavery and trafficking risk order containing a prohibition within subsection (2)(c).

(6) Subsection (5) does not apply in relation to—

(a) a passport issued by or on behalf of the authorities of a country outside the United Kingdom if the passport has been returned to those authorities;

(b) a passport issued by or on behalf of an international organisation if the passport has been returned to that organisation.

24. Variation, renewal and discharge

(1) A person within subsection (2) may by complaint to a magistrates' court apply for an order varying, renewing or discharging a slavery and trafficking risk order.

(2) The persons are—

(a) the defendant;

(b) the chief officer of police for the area in which the defendant lives;

(c) a chief officer of police who believes that the defendant is in, or is intending to come to, that officer's police area;

(d) where the order was made on an application by a chief officer of police, that officer.

(3) On the application the court, after hearing—

(a) the person making the application, and

(b) the other persons mentioned in subsection (2) (if they wish to be heard), may make any order varying, renewing or discharging the slavery and trafficking risk order that the court considers appropriate.

(4) An order may be renewed, or varied so as to impose additional prohibitions on the defendant, only if the court is satisfied that it is necessary to do so for the purpose of protecting persons generally, or particular persons, from physical or psychological harm caused by the defendant committing an offence under Part 1.

(5) Any renewed or varied order may contain only those prohibitions which the court is satisfied are necessary for that purpose.

(6) The court must not discharge an order before the end of 2 years beginning with the day on which the order was made, without the consent of the defendant and—

(a) where the application is made by the defendant, the chief officer of police for the area in which the defendant lives;

(b) where the application is made by a chief officer of police, that chief officer.

25. Interim slavery and trafficking risk orders

(1) This section applies where an application for a slavery and trafficking risk order ("the main application") has not been determined.

(2) An application for an order under this section (an "interim slavery and trafficking risk order")—

(a) may be made by the complaint by which the main application is made, or

(b) if the main application has been made, may be made by the person who has made that application, by complaint to the court to which that application has been made.

(3) The court may, if it considers it just to do so, make an interim slavery and trafficking risk order, prohibiting the defendant from doing anything described in the order.

(4) Such an order—

(a) has effect only for a fixed period, specified in the order;

(b) ceases to have effect, if it has not already done so, on the determination of the main application.

(5) The applicant or the defendant may by complaint apply to the court that made the interim slavery and trafficking risk order for the order to be varied, renewed or discharged.

26. Appeals

(1) A defendant may appeal to the Crown Court—

(a) against the making of a slavery and trafficking risk order;

(b) against the making of an interim slavery and trafficking risk order;

(c) against the making of an order under section 24, or the refusal to make such an order.

(2) The Crown Court may make such orders as may be necessary to give effect to its determination of the appeal, and may also make such incidental or consequential orders as appear to it to be just.

(3) An order made by the Crown Court on an appeal against the making of an interim slavery and trafficking risk order is to be treated for the purposes of section 25(5) as if it were an order of the court from which the appeal was brought.

(4) Subsection (3) does not apply to an order directing that an application be re- heard by a magistrates' court.

27. Offences

(1) A person who, without reasonable excuse, does anything that the person is prohibited from doing by—

(a) a slavery and trafficking risk order, or

(b) an interim slavery and trafficking risk order, commits an offence.

(2) A person commits an offence if, without reasonable excuse, the person fails to comply with a requirement imposed under section 23(4).

(3) A person guilty of an offence under this section is liable—

(a) on conviction on indictment, to imprisonment for a term not exceeding 5 years,

(b) on summary conviction, to imprisonment for a term not exceeding 6 months or a fine not exceeding £5,000 or both.

(4) Where a person is convicted of an offence under this section, it is not open to the court by or before which the person is convicted to make an order for conditional discharge in respect of the offence.

28. Guidance

(1) The Secretary of State must issue guidance to chief officers of police and to the Director General of the National Crime Agency in relation to the exercise by them of their powers with regard to slavery and trafficking risk orders and interim slavery and trafficking risk orders.

(2) The Secretary of State may, from time to time, revise the guidance issued under subsection (1).

(3) The Secretary of State must arrange for any guidance issued or revised under this section to be published in a way the Secretary of State considers appropriate.

Interpretation of Part 2

29. Interpretation of Part 2

(1) In this Part—

"cautioned" means cautioned after the person concerned has admitted the offence,

"country" includes territory,

"interim slavery and trafficking prevention order" means an order under section 17,

"interim slavery and trafficking risk order" means an order under section 25,

"slavery or human trafficking offence" means an offence listed in the Schedule,

"slavery and trafficking prevention order" means an order under section 11 or 12,

"slavery and trafficking risk order" means an order under section 21,

"UK national" has the same meaning as in Part 1.

(2) In this Part "passport" means—

(a) a United Kingdom passport within the meaning of the Immigration Act 1971;

(b) a passport issued by or on behalf of the authorities of a country outside the United Kingdom, or by or on behalf of an international organisation;

(c) a document that can be used (in some or all circumstances) instead of a passport.

(3) In this Part a reference to a conviction includes a conviction for an offence in respect of which an order for conditional discharge is made, despite—

(a) section 14(1) of the Powers of Criminal Courts (Sentencing) Act 2000 (conviction with conditional discharge deemed not to be a conviction),

(b) article 6(1) of the Criminal Justice (Northern Ireland) Order 1996 (S.I. 1996/3160 (N.I. 24)) (equivalent provision for Northern Ireland).

(4) Subsection (3) applies only to convictions after this Part comes into force.

(5) In this Part a reference to a conviction includes a finding of a court in summary proceedings that the accused did the act charged, where the court makes an order under—

(a) section 37(3) of the Mental Health Act 1983,

(b) section 58(3) of the Criminal Procedure (Scotland) Act 1995, or

(c) article 44(4) of the Mental Health (Northern Ireland) Order 1986 (S.I. 1986/595 (N.I. 4)), (hospital and guardianship orders).

(6) In relation to an offence under the law of Scotland, a reference in this Part to a person being found not guilty by reason of insanity is to be treated as a reference to a person being acquitted by reason of the special defence in section 51A of the Criminal Procedure (Scotland) Act 1995.

(7) In this Part, a reference to a finding that a person is under a disability and has done the act charged against the person in respect of an offence includes a finding that a person is insane or unfit to be tried and has done the act charged against the person in respect of an offence.

Section 127 of the Magistrates Courts Act 1980 (time limits) does not apply to a complaint under any provision of this Part.

PART 3
THE ANTI-SLAVERY COMMISSIONER

30. The Anti-slavery Commissioner

(1) The Secretary of State must appoint a person as the Anti-slavery Commissioner (in this Part "the Commissioner").

(2) The Commissioner is to hold office in accordance with the terms of the Commissioner's appointment.

(3) The Secretary of State may pay in respect of the Commissioner any expenses, remuneration or allowances that the Secretary of State may determine.

(4) The Secretary of State may, after consultation with the Commissioner, provide the Commissioner with—

(a) such staff, and

(b) such accommodation, equipment and other facilities, as the Secretary of State considers necessary for the exercise of the Commissioner's functions.

(5) In Part 3 of Schedule 1 to the House of Commons Disqualification Act 1975 (offices disqualifying for membership: other disqualifying offices) at the appropriate place insert—"Anti-slavery Commissioner".

(6) In Part 6 of Schedule 1 to the Freedom of Information Act 2000 (other public bodies and offices: general) at the appropriate place insert— "The Anti-slavery Commissioner".

31. General functions of Commissioner

(1) The Commissioner must encourage good practice in the prevention, detection, investigation and prosecution of offences under Part 1.

(2) The things that the Commissioner may do in pursuance of subsection (1) include—

(a) making reports to the Secretary of State on any permitted matter;

(b) making recommendations to any public authority about the exercise of its functions in England and Wales;

(c) undertaking or supporting (financially or otherwise) the carrying out of research;

(d) providing information, education or training;

(e) consulting people.

(3) In subsection (2)(a) "permitted matter" means a matter which—

(a) the Secretary of State has authorised the Commissioner to report on, or

(b) the current annual plan, approved by the Secretary of State under section 32(3), states is a matter the Commissioner proposes to report on.

(4) The Commissioner must (after ascertaining whether the Secretary of State wishes to exercise the power conferred by subsection (5)) publish each report made to the Secretary of State under subsection (2)(a).

(5) The Secretary of State may direct the Commissioner to omit from any report before publication any material whose publication the Secretary of State thinks—

(a) is undesirable for reasons of national security,

(b) might jeopardise an individual's safety, or

(c) might prejudice the investigation or prosecution of an offence.

(6) In this section "public authority" means any public authority within the meaning of section 6 of the Human Rights Act 1998 (other than a court or tribunal) which exercises functions in England and Wales.

32. Annual plans and annual reports

(1) Before the beginning of each calendar year the Commissioner must—

(a) prepare an annual plan setting out how the Commissioner proposes to exercise the Commissioner's functions during the year, and

(b) submit the annual plan to the Secretary of State for approval.

(2) An annual plan must in particular—

(a) state the Commissioner's objectives and priorities for the year;

(b) state any matters on which the Commissioner proposes to report under section 31(2)(a) during the year;

(c) state any other activities the Commissioner proposes to undertake during the year in the exercise of the Commissioner's functions.

(3) The Secretary of State may approve an annual plan either without modifications or with modifications agreed with the Commissioner.

(4) As soon as reasonably practicable after the end of each calendar year the Commissioner must submit to the Secretary of State an annual report on the exercise of the Commissioner's functions during the year.

(5) An annual report must include—

(a) an assessment of the extent to which the Commissioner's objectives and priorities for the year have been met;

(b) a statement of the matters on which the Commissioner has reported under section 31(2)(a) during the year;

(c) a statement of the other activities the Commissioner has undertaken during the year in the exercise of the Commissioner's functions.

(6) The Secretary of State must lay before Parliament—

(a) any annual plan the Secretary of State approves; (b) any annual report the Secretary of State receives.

(7) But before laying an annual report before Parliament the Secretary of State may remove from the report any material whose publication the Secretary of State thinks—

(a) is undesirable for reasons of national security,

(b) might jeopardise an individual's safety, or

(c) might prejudice the investigation or prosecution of an offence.

33. Duty to co-operate with Commissioner

(1) The Commissioner may request a specified public authority to co-operate with the Commissioner in any way that the Commissioner considers necessary for the purposes of the Commissioner's functions.

(2) A specified public authority must so far as reasonably practicable comply with a request made to it under this section.

(3) A public authority which discloses information to the Commissioner in pursuance of subsection (2) does not breach—

(a) any obligation of confidence owed by the public authority, or

(b) any other restriction on the disclosure of information (however imposed).

(4) But subsection (2) does not require or authorise any disclosure of information which—

(a) contravenes the Data Protection Act 1998, or

(b) is prohibited by Part 1 of the Regulation of Investigatory Powers Act 2000.

(5) In this section—

"public authority" has the same meaning as in section 31;

"specified public authority" means a public authority which is specified in, or is of a description specified in, an order made by the Secretary of State for the purposes of this section.

34. Restriction on exercise of functions

The Commissioner must not exercise any function in relation to—

(a) a particular offence;

(b) the initiation or conduct of a particular investigation or particular proceedings;

(c) anything done or omitted to be done by a person acting in a judicial capacity or on the instructions of or on behalf of such a person.

PART 4

MISCELLANEOUS

Duty to notify NCA

35. Duty to notify NCA about suspected victims of human trafficking

(1) A specified public authority must notify the National Crime Agency if it has reasonable grounds to suspect that an individual may be a victim of human trafficking.

(2) The Secretary of State may by order make provision determining the information that must be included in a notification under this section.

(3) Provision made under subsection (2) may not require information to be included in a notification if its inclusion would result in a disclosure which contravenes the Data Protection Act 1998.

(4) The Secretary of State may issue guidance to specified public authorities as to the sorts of things which indicate that an individual may be a victim of human trafficking.

(5) For the purposes of this section an individual is a "victim of human trafficking" if the individual is— (a) a victim of an offence under section 2, or

(b) a victim of conduct which would have constituted an offence under that section had the person responsible for the conduct been a UK national.

In this section—

"public authority" means any public authority within the meaning of section 6 of the Human Rights Act 1998 (other than a court or

tribunal) which exercises functions in England and Wales;

"specified" means specified in an order made by the Secretary of State for the purposes of this section;

"UK national" has the same meaning as in Part 1.

Final provisions

36. Saving, transitional and consequential provision

(1) The Secretary of State may by order make whatever saving, transitory or transitional provision the Secretary of State thinks appropriate in connection with the coming into force of any provision of this Act or of an order made under this Act.

(2) The Secretary of State may by order make whatever provision the Secretary of State thinks appropriate in consequence of this Act.

(3) The provision which may be made by an order under subsection (2) includes provision amending, repealing or revoking any provision of an Act or of subordinate legislation (within the meaning of the Interpretation Act 1978).

37. Orders

(1) Any power of the Secretary of State to make an order under this Act is exercisable by statutory instrument.

(2) A statutory instrument containing an order under this Act is subject to annulment in pursuance of a resolution of either House of Parliament, subject to subsections (3) and (4).

(3) Subsection (2) does not apply to a statutory instrument containing—

(a) only orders under section 36(1) (transitional etc. provision) or section 39 (commencement);

(b) an order under section 36(2) which amends or repeals any provision of an Act.

(4) A statutory instrument containing an order under section 36(2) which amends or repeals any provision of an Act may not be made unless a draft of the instrument has been laid before, and approved by a resolution of, each House of Parliament.

38. Extent

This Act extends to England and Wales only.

39. Commencement

(1) Sections 36 to 40 come into force on the day on which this Act is passed.

(2) The other provisions of this Act come into force on whatever day or days the Secretary of State appoints by order.

Different days may be appointed for different purposes.

40. Short title

This Act may be cited as the Modern Slavery Act 2014.

Section 11
SLAVERY AND HUMAN TRAFFICKING OFFENCES

Nationality, Immigration and Asylum Act 2002 (c. 41)

1.An offence under section 145 of the Nationality, Immigration and Asylum Act 2002 (trafficking for prostitution).

Sexual Offences Act 2003 (c. 42)

2 (1) An offence under section 57, 58, 58A, 59 or 59A of the Sexual Offences Act 2003 (trafficking for sexual exploitation).

(2) An offence under section 62 of that Act (committing offence with intent to commit relevant sexual offence), where the relevant sexual offence the person in question intended to commit was an offence under section 57, 58, 58A, 59 or 59A of that Act.

Criminal Justice (Scotland) Act 2003 (asp 7)

3. An offence under section 22 of the Criminal Justice (Scotland) Act 2003 (trafficking for prostitution).

Asylum and Immigration (Treatment of Claimants, etc.) Act 2004 (c. 19)

4. An offence under section 4 of the Asylum and Immigration (Treatment of Claimants, etc.) Act 2004 (trafficking for exploitation).

Coroners and Justice Act 2009 (c. 25)

5. An offence under section 71 of the Coroners and Justice Act 2009 (slavery, servitude and forced or compulsory labour).

Criminal Justice and Licensing (Scotland) Act 2010 (asp 13)

6. An offence under section 47 of the Criminal Justice and Licensing (Scotland) Act 2010 (slavery, servitude and forced or compulsory labour).

Modern Slavery Act 2014

7. An offence under Part 1 of this Act.

Ancillary offences

8. (1) An offence of attempting or conspiring to commit an offence listed in this Schedule.

(2) An offence of aiding, abetting, counselling, procuring or inciting the commission of an offence listed in this Schedule.

(3) An offence under Part 2 of the Serious Crime Act 2007 (encouraging or assisting) where the offence (or one of the offences) which the person in question intends or believes would be committed is an offence listed in this Schedule.

4. Explanatory Notes

Draft Modern Slavery Bill

Introduction

1. These Explanatory Notes relate to the draft Modern Slavery Bill as Published on 16 December 2013 for pre-legislative scrutiny by a Joint Committee of both Houses of Parliament. They have been prepared by the Home Office in order to assist the reader of the draft Bill and to help inform

debate on it. They do not form part of the draft Bill and have not been endorsed by Parliament.

2. The Notes need to be read in conjunction with the draft Bill. They are not, and are not meant to be, a comprehensive description of the draft Bill. So where a clause or part of a clause does not seem to require any explanation or comment, none is given.

Summary

3. The Bill is in four parts. Part 1 consolidates the current offences of slavery and human trafficking whilst increasing the maximum penalty for such offences. Part 2 provides for two new civil preventative orders, the Slavery and Trafficking Prevention Order and the Slavery and Trafficking Risk Order. Part 3 establishes the office of Anti-slavery Commissioner and sets out the functions of the Commissioner. Part 4 introduces a duty on specified public authorities to notify the National Crime Agency about suspected victims of human trafficking and makes general provisions.

Background

4. Human trafficking is a brutal form of organised crime in which people are treated as commodities and exploited for criminal gain. The true extent of human trafficking in the United Kingdom, and indeed globally, is unknown. This is an international problem and victims may have entered the United Kingdom legally, on forged documentation or clandestinely, or they may be British citizens living in the United Kingdom. Modern slavery takes a number of forms, including sexual exploitation, forced labour and domestic servitude, and victims come from all walks of life. Victims are often unwilling to come forward to law enforcement or public protection agencies, not seeing themselves as victims, or fearing further reprisals from their traffickers, and/ or may not always be recognised as trafficking victims by those who come into contact with them. In particular, there may be particular social and cultural barriers to men identifying themselves as victims.

5. The Government has outlined its approach to modern slavery within the Serious and Organised Crime Strategy.[9] The Inter-Departmental Ministerial Group on Human Trafficking also published its annual report[10] in October 2013 which highlights activity to fight modern slavery across the UK, as well as providing information on the nature and scale of the problem.

6. The intention to introduce a Modern Slavery Bill was announced by the Home Secretary on the 25 August 2013. The Home Secretary subsequently announced a series of evidence sessions[11] to gather information to support pre-

legislative scrutiny of the draft Bill, lead by Frank Field MP. A report from the evidence sessions was published on 16 December. To ensure the Bill is also informed by international best practice and the challenges faced in key source and transit countries, Anthony Steen, Chair of the Human Trafficking Foundation, was also commissioned as the Home Secretary's special envoy to report back on a series of international visits.

Territorial Extent and Application

7. The provisions of the draft Bill extend to England and Wales only at present. In relation to Wales the provisions of the Bill generally related to reserved matters, namely preventing and detecting the crimes of slavery and human trafficking so are not within the competence of the Welsh Government. However, discussions continue with the Welsh Government on the Bill and its effect on public authorities in Wales.

8. The Government is in discussion with the Scottish Government and Northern Ireland Department of Justice as to whether some or all of the provisions of the Bill, as introduced, should extend to Scotland and Northern Ireland respectively.

Commentary on Clauses

Part 1: Offences of Slavery and Human Trafficking

9. Part 1 makes provision for the consolidation of the current offences of slavery and human trafficking into one Act. Currently, a trafficking offence is an offence under section 59A of the Sexual Offences Act 2003 or section 4 of the Asylum and Immigration (Treatment of Claimants, etc.) Act 2004. An offence of forced labour, slavery or servitude is an offence under section 71 of the Coroners and Justice Act 2009.

10. The primary rationale for retaining two offences is that they concern different types of conduct. The physical element of the offence of human trafficking is the actual movement of a victim but with intent to exploit them, whether for sexual exploitation for forced labour or otherwise. Whereas, in the slavery offence in clause 1 the physical element is actual slavery or forced labour.

11. Currently, the maximum sentence for slavery or trafficking offences is 14 years imprisonment. To reflect the serious nature of these crimes, the Bill increases the maximum penalties on conviction for either offence to life imprisonment. The offences will also be included in the extended determinate sentences regime. This will make them one of a number of serious offences

where, on conviction of a second offence, an individual would automatically be considered for a life sentence.

Clause 1: Slavery, Servitude and Forced or Compulsory Labour

12. *Subsection (1)* provides for an offence of slavery, servitude and forced or compulsory labour. It replaces the existing such offence in section 71 of the Coroners and Justice Act 2009 which is repealed by clause 10. The wording of the offence has not been amended and continues to criminalise slavery, servitude and forced or compulsory labour.

13. *Subsection (2)* requires subsection (1) to be interpreted in accordance with Article 4 of the ECHR. That Article states:

1) No one shall be held in slavery or servitude.

2) No one shall be required to perform forced or compulsory labour.

3) For the purpose of this Article the term "forced or compulsory labour" shall not include:

a) any work required to be done in the ordinary course of detention imposed according to the provisions of Article 5 of this Convention or during conditional release from such detention;

b) any service of a military character or, in case of conscientious objectors in countries where they are recognised, service exacted instead of compulsory military service;

c) any service exacted in case of an emergency or calamity threatening the life or well-being of the community;

d) any work or service which forms part of normal civic obligations.

Clause 2: Human Trafficking

14. This clause provides for a single offence of human trafficking covering sexual and non-sexual exploitation. It replaces the two existing offences in sections 59A of the Sexual Offences Act 2003 (which relates to human trafficking for the purposes of sexual exploitation), as inserted by section 109 of the Protection of Freedoms Act 2012 (which replaced the previous offences in sections 57 to 59 of the Sexual offences Act 2003), and section 4 of the Asylum and Immigration (Treatment of Claimants, etc) Act 2004 (which relates to human trafficking for the purposes of labour or other exploitation); both these existing offences are repealed by clause 10. Introducing one offence for all types of trafficking will make it administratively simpler for investigators and prosecutors to bring forward human trafficking prosecutions.

15. *Subsection (1)* makes it a criminal offence to intentionally arrange or facilitate the rrival in or entry into (paragraph (a)), departure from (paragraph (b)), or travel within (paragraph (c)) the UK or any other country of another person with a view to their being exploited.

16. *Subsection (2)* highlights that for the purpose of an human trafficking offence the victim's consent to their transportation is irrelevant.

17. *Subsection (3)* provides that the arranging or facilitating is done with a view to the exploitation of the victim (V) if the perpetrator (P) either intends to exploit V, or believes that any other person is likely to exploit V. It is irrelevant where in the world that exploitation might take place.

18. *Subsection (4)* makes the offence extra-territorial in its reach in relation to UK nationals. It provides that a UK national commits an offence regardless of where in the world the arranging or facilitating takes place or regardless of which country is the country of arrival, entry, travel or departure. For example, a UK national who trafficks a person from Spain to France could be prosecuted in England and Wales for this offence.

19. *Subsection (5)* provides for more limited extra-territoriality in relation to a non-UK national. Such a person commits the offence if any part of the arranging or facilitating takes place in the UK or if the UK is the country of arrival, entry, travel or departure.

Clause 3: Meaning of Exploitation

20. The clause 2 offence is arranging of facilitating travel with a view to the victim's exploitation. This clause sets out the meaning of exploitation for the purposes of clause 2.

21. *Subsection (2)* covers slavery, servitude and forced or compulsory labour by reference to the offence under section 1.

22. *Subsection (3)* covers sexual exploitation by reference to conduct which would constitute the commission of an offence of taking, or permitting to take, indecent photographs of children or any of the sexual offences provided for in Part 1 of the Sexual Offences Act 2003 (these include offences relating to rape, sexual assault, prostitution and child pornography). *Subsection (3)(b)* ensures that equivalent conduct committed outside of England and Wales also comes within the definition even though for jurisdictional reasons it would not be an offence under English law.

23. *Subsection (4)* covers exploitation in the context of trafficking for the sale and purchase of organs and human material more generally (subject to certain exceptions) by reference to the offences in the Human Tissue Act 2004.

24. *Subsection (5)* covers all other types of exploitation where a person is forced, threatened or deceived into providing a service of any kind, providing a person with benefits or enabling another to acquire benefits. This includes forcing a person to engage in activities such as begging or shop theft. It is not necessary for this conduct to be a criminal offence.

25. *Subsection (6)* also covers exploitation where a person provides services or benefits or enables another person to acquire benefits. However, in this subsection force threats or deception are not required. Rather, it provides it is exploitation where a person is used to do something, having been chosen on the grounds that he or she is ill, disabled, young or related to a person, in circumstances where a person without the illness, disability, youth or family relationship would be likely to refuse.

Clause 4: Committing Offence with Intent

26. This clause provides that it is an offence to commit another offence with a view to committing a trafficking offence under clause 2. This separate offence ensures that the preparatory criminal conduct for a lesser offence, for example theft of a vehicle with the intention of using that vehicle to traffick individuals, can attract the higher penalties provided for in clause 5.

Clause 5: Penalties

27. This clause sets out the maximum penalties for the offences in clauses 1, 2 and 4.

28. *Subsection (1)* provides that the maximum sentence for a clause 1 or 2 offence is six months imprisonment (increasing to 12 months when the increase in magistrates' courts sentencing powers provided for in the Criminal Justice Act 2003 are brought into force) or an unlimited fine, or both in the case of a summary conviction and life imprisonment for conviction on indictment. This compares with a maximum of 14 years imprisonment for the existing slavery and human trafficking offences.

29. *Subsections (2) and (3)* provide for the maximum penalties for the clause 4 offence. In most instances the maximum is six months imprisonment (again increasing to 12 months when the increase in magistrates' courts sentencing powers are brought into force) or an unlimited fine, or both in the case of a summary conviction and 10 years imprisonment for conviction on indictment. However, where the precursor offence committed under clause 4 is one of kidnapping or false imprisonment, the maximum penalty is life imprisonment.

Clause 6: Sentencing

30. This clause adds the clause 1 and 2 offences to the list of offences in Part 1 of Schedule 15B to the Criminal Justice Act 2003 ("the 2003 Act"). The effect is to engage the provisions in sections 224A, 226A(2) and 246A(2)(b) of the 2003 Act. By virtue of the provisions in section 224A of the 2003 Act, a court must impose a life sentence on a person aged 18 or over who is convicted of an offence listed in Part 1 of Schedule 15B to that Act which is serious enough to justify a sentence of imprisonment of 10 years or more, if that person has previously been convicted of an offence listed in any Part of Schedule 15B and was sentenced to imprisonment for life or for a period of 10 years or more in respect of that previous offence. However, the court is not obliged to impose a life sentence where it is of the opinion that there are particular circumstances which relate to the offence, the previous offence or the offender which would make it unjust to do so in all the circumstances.

31. Section 226A provides for extended sentences for adults. The sentence may be imposed in respect of the sexual and violent offences listed in Schedule 15 to the 2003 Act where certain conditions are met. The court must consider that the offender presents a substantial risk of causing serious harm through re-offending. In addition the court must either consider that the current offence is serious enough to merit a determinate sentence of at least 4 years, or at the time the present offence was committed the offender must have previously been convicted of an offence listed in Schedule 15B of the 2003 Act (which will now include the slavery and human trafficking offences). Where these conditions are made out, the court may impose an extended period for which the offender is to be subject to a licence of up to five years for a violent offence and up to eight years for a sexual offence. Schedule 15 to the 2003 Act lists violent and sexual offences separately.

32. Section 246A of the 2003 Act deals with the release arrangements in respect of persons sentenced to an extended sentence under section 226A of that Act. Offenders who have committed an offence listed in Parts 1 to 3 of Schedule 15B to the 2003 Act (Part 1 will now include the slavery and human trafficking offences), or whose offending merits a custodial term of 10 years or more, will be considered for release on licence by the Parole Board once the offender has served two-thirds of the appropriate custodial term, and will be released automatically at the end of the appropriate custodial term (that is, the term imposed by the court as the custodial element of the extended sentence) if the Parole Board has not already directed release.

Clause 7: Forfeiture of Land Vehicle, Ship or Aircraft

33. This clause enables the court, when a person is convicted on indictment of a human trafficking offence under clause 2, to order the forfeiture of a vehicle, ship or aircraft used or intended to be used in connection with the offence of which the person is convicted. *Subsection (2)* lists the circumstances that would allow the forfeiture of a vehicle; *subsections (3) to (5)* do likewise for a ship or aircraft. *Subsection (6)* allows a person who claims to have an interest in a vehicle, ship or aircraft, and who makes an application to the court, to make representations on the question of forfeiture before the court may make an order for its forfeiture. Similar provisions are currently contained in section 60A of the Sexual Offences Act 2003 and supplement the more general provisions on forfeiture in section 143 of the Powers of the Criminal Courts (Sentencing) Act 2000.

Clause 8: Detention of Land Vehicles, Ship or Aircraft

34. *Subsections (1) to (3)* enable a constable or immigration officer not below the rank of chief immigration officer to detain a vehicle, ship or aircraft of a person arrested for an offence under clause 2 if it is one which the constable or officer concerned has reasonable grounds for believing could, on conviction of the arrested person for the offence for which he was arrested, be the subject of an order for forfeiture made under clause 7. Detention is permitted until a decision is taken whether or not to charge the arrested person, until the arrested person is acquitted, the charge against him dismissed or the proceedings discontinued, or, where the person is subsequently convicted, until the court makes a decision on forfeiture.

35. *Subsection (4)* lists the circumstances in which a person other than the arrested person may apply to the court for the release of that vehicle, ship or aircraft. *Subsection (5)* provides that on such an application the court may release the vehicle, ship or aircraft subject to satisfactory security or surety and on condition that it is made available to the court if the arrested person is convicted and if an order under clause 7 is made. Similar provisions are currently contained in section 60B of the Sexual Offences Act 2003.

Clause 9: Interpretation of Part 1

36. This clause defines terms used in Part 1.

Clause 10: Repeals of Existing Provisions

37. This clause repeals the legislation containing the existing slavery and human trafficking offences and related provisions.

Part 2: Prevention Orders

38. Part 2 makes provision (clauses 11 to 29)for the introduction of new civil orders to enable prohibitions to be imposed by the courts on individuals convicted of a slavery or trafficking offence, or those involved in slavery or trafficking but who have not been convicted of a slavery or trafficking offence. The rationale for creating these orders is to enable law enforcement bodies and the courts to take tougher action against those involved in trafficking, and to protect individuals from the harm caused by slavery or trafficking by preventing future offending. Slavery and trafficking are high-harm activities, which adversely affect the rights and freedoms of those who are victims of them. The new orders will complement existing civil orders[12], enabling the courts to impose necessary prohibitions on individuals where there is evidence of that individual posing a risk of causing another person to be the victim of slavery, or trafficking for exploitation.

Clause 11: Slavery and Trafficking Prevention Orders on Sentencing

39. This clause provides for slavery and trafficking prevention orders ("STPO") on conviction. *Subsection (1)* enables a court (for example, the magistrates' court, youth court, Crown Court or in limited cases the Court of Appeal) to impose a STPO on a person on a conviction or other finding in respect of that person for a slavery or human trafficking offence. A slavery or human trafficking offence means an offence listed in the *Schedule* (introduced by *subsection (3)*) to the Bill. The Schedule lists the new offences provided for in Part 1 of the Bill, preceding offences in England and Wales and equivalent offences in Scotland and Northern Ireland Since the Bill extends only to England and Wales the power conferred by this clause will be available only where a court in England and Wales deals with a person for an offence under the law of England and Wales. Offences under the law of Scotland and Northern Ireland are however relevant to whether a court in England and Wales may make an order under clause 12.

40. *Subsection (2)* provides that the court must be satisfied that it is necessary to impose a STPO for the purposes of protecting persons generally, or particular persons, from physical or psychological harm caused by the offender committing an offence in Part 1.

41. *Subsection (4)* provides that a STPO may be made in relation to a conviction and finding made before this clause comes into force.

Clause 12: Slavery and Trafficking Prevention on Application

42. This clause provides for a STPO in cases other than on conviction etc. An application for a STPO may be made to a magistrates' court by a chief officer of police or the Director General of the National Crime Agency ("NCA") (*subsection (1)*). The NCA, established under section 1 of the Crime and Courts Act 2013, holds the national lead for tackling slavery and human trafficking. Where an application is made by the Director General of the NCA, the Director General must notify the chief officer of police for the area where the offender resides or is believed to intend to reside (*subsection (4)*).

43. The court in accordance with *subsection (2)* must be satisfied that the person is a relevant offender (defined in clause 13) and that, since the individual became a relevant offender, he or she has acted in a way which makes it necessary to impose an order for the purposes of protecting persons generally, or particular persons, from physical or psychological harm caused by the offender committing an offence in Part 1.

44. *Subsection (5)* provides that an application is made by complaint.

45. *Subsection (6)* provides that an application for a STPO under this clause may be made in relation to conduct that took place before its commencement.

Clause 13. Meaning of "Relevant Offender"

46. *Subsections (1) to (2)* define a relevant offender for the purposes of clause 12. A relevant offender includes a person convicted, made the subject of a finding or cautioned for a slavery or human trafficking offence in any part of the United Kingdom, and also a person convicted etc. in relation to an equivalent offence outside the United Kingdom (defined in *subsections (3) to (5)*). Where an application is made in respect of an equivalent offence, it is open to the person in respect of whom the application is made to challenge whether the offence he or she has been convicted of is an equivalent offence. They can do this by serving a notice on the applicant setting out the grounds for such a challenge (*subsection (6)*), or without serving such a notice if the court permits.

Clause 14: Effect of Slavery and Trafficking Prevention Orders

47. *Subsection (1)* provides that a STPO may prohibit the person in respect of whom the order is made from doing anything described in it. The nature of any prohibition is a matter for the court to determine. A prohibition may include preventing a person from participating in a particular type of business, operating as a gangmaster, visiting a particular place, working with

children or travelling to a specified country. The court may only include in an order prohibitions which it is satisfied are necessary for the purpose of protecting persons generally, or particular persons, from physical or psychological harm caused by the offender committing an offence under Part 1 (*subsection (2)*).

48. *Subsections (3) and (4)* provide for the duration of a STPO and the prohibitions in it. A STPO may last for a fixed period of at least five years or until further order. The prohibitions specified in it may each have different duration.

Clause 15: Prohibitions on Foreign Travel

49. A STPO may prohibit a person from travelling to any specified country outside the United Kingdom, any country other than a country specified in the order or any country outside the United Kingdom (*subsection (2)*). Such a prohibition may be for a fixed period not exceeding five years, but may be renewed at the end of that period (*subsections (1) and (3)*). A person prohibited from travelling to any country must surrender all his or her passports to the police (*subsection (4)*). The police must return any such passports, unless they have been returned to the relevant national or international issuing authorities, once the all-country prohibition ceases to have effect (*subsections (5) and (6)*).

Clause 16: Variation, Renewal and Discharge

50. This clause makes provision to enable a person in respect of whom a STPO has been made or the police to apply to the court which made the order to vary, renew or discharge the order (*subsections (1) and (2)*). This provision ensures that the order can be modified to reflect changing circumstances, both to ensure that it remains effective to manage the risk posed by activities relating to slavery or trafficking and that the order remains necessary for that purpose.

51. The person in respect of whom the order was made and the police have the right to be heard by the court (*subsection (4)*). In relation to the imposition of any additional prohibitions, the court must apply the same test as that which it applied when making the order (*subsection (5)*). An order may not be discharged within five years of it being made without the consent of the relevant chief officer of police (*subsection (7)*).

Clause 17: Interim Slavery and Trafficking Prevention Orders

52. *Subsections (1) and (2)* provide for an interim STPO to be made where an application has been made for a STPO under clause 12 and the court considers that it is just to do so (*subsection (3)*). For example, the court may make an interim order in a case where it is satisfied that this is necessary for the purpose of protecting a person from immediate harm pending the full determination of the application for the order.

53. An interim order must be made for a specified period and ceases to have effect once the main application has been determined (*subsection (4)*). An interim order may be varied, renewed or discharged (*subsection (5)*).

Clause 18: Appeals

54. A person may appeal against the making of a STPO on conviction in the same manner as an appeal against sentence (*subsection (1)(a) and (b)*). For example, an order made by the magistrates' court may be appealed to the Crown Court. A STPO made on an application under clause 12 and an interim STPO may be appealed to the Crown Court (*subsection (1)(c) and (2)*).

55. A person in respect of whom an order is made may also appeal a decision under clause 16 to vary, renew or discharge an order (*subsection (3)*).

56. Subsection (4) sets out the powers of the Crown Court when determining an appeal. It will be open to the court to revoke the order or to amend its provision (either the duration or the prohibitions contained in it).

Clause 19: Offences

57. *Subsection (1)* makes it an offence for a person to do anything which is prohibited by a STPO or an interim STPO without reasonable excuse.

58. Where an order includes a foreign travel prohibition in respect of all countries outside the United Kingdom, *subsection (2)* makes it an offence for the person subject to the order to fail, without reasonable excuse, to surrender all his or her passports.

59. The maximum penalty for either offence is six months imprisonment or a fine of £5,000 or both on summary conviction, or five years imprisonment following conviction on indictment (*subsection (3)*). *Subsection (4)* precludes the court from making an order for a conditional discharge following a conviction for an offence in this clause.

Clause 20: Guidance

60. This clause confers a duty on the Secretary of State to issue guidance to chief officers and the Director General of the NCA in relation to their

powers to apply for STPOs and interim STPOs (*subsection (1)*). The Secretary of State may issue revised guidance (*subsection (2)*). The Secretary of State is required to publish such guidance (*subsection (3)*); it is not subject to any parliamentary procedure.

Clause 21: Slavery and Trafficking Risk Orders

61. *Subsection (1)* enables a magistrates' court to make a slavery and trafficking risk order ("STRO") on an application by a chief officer of police or the Director General of the NCA. A STRO may be made against either an adult or person under 18. Where an application is made by the Director General of the NCA, the Director General must notify the chief officer of police for the area where the offender resides or is believed to intend to reside (*subsection (4)*).

62. *Subsection (2)* sets out the test for making a STRO, namely that the court is satisfied that the person in respect of whom the order is sought has acted in a way which makes it necessary to make an order for the purposes of protecting persons generally, or particular persons, from physical or psychological harm caused by the offender committing an offence in Part 1. There is no requirement for the person in respect of whom an order is sought to have previously been convicted or cautioned in relation to a criminal offence.

63. *Subsection (5)* provides that an application for a STRO is made by complaint.

64. *Subsection (6)* provides that an application for a STRO may be made in relation to conduct that took place before the commencement of this clause.

Clause 22: Effect of Slavery and Trafficking Risk Orders

65. *Subsection (1)* provides that a STRO may prohibit the person in respect of whom the order is made from doing anything described in it. The nature of any prohibition is a matter for the court to determine. A prohibition may include preventing a person from participating in a particular type of business, operating as a gangmaster, visiting a particular place, working with children or travelling to a specified country. The court may only include in an order prohibitions which it is satisfied are necessary for the purpose of protecting persons generally, or particular persons, from physical or psychological harm caused by the offender committing an offence under Part 1 (*subsection (2)*).

66. *Subsections (3) and (4)* provide for the duration of a STRO and the prohibitions in it. A STRO may last for a fixed period of at least two years or

until further order. The prohibitions specified in it may each have different duration.

Clause 23: Prohibitions on Foreign Travel

67. A STRO may prohibit a person from travelling to any specified country outside the United Kingdom, from travelling to any country other than a country specified in the order or from travelling to any country outside the United Kingdom (*subsection (2)*). Such a prohibition may be for a fixed period not exceeding five years, but may be renewed at the end of that period (*subsections (1) and (3)*). A person prohibited from travelling to any country must surrender all his or her passports to the police (*subsection (4)*). The police must return any such passports, unless they have been returned to the relevant national or international issuing authorities, once the all-country prohibition ceases to have effect (*subsections (5) and (6)*).

Clause 24: Variation, Renewal and Discharge

68. This clause makes provision to enable the person who is subject to a STRO or the police to apply to a magistrates' court to vary, renew or discharge the order (*subsections (1) and (2)*). This provision ensures that the order can be modified to reflect changing circumstances, both to ensure that it remains effective to manage the risk posed by activities related to slavery or trafficking and that the order remains necessary for that purpose.

69. The person in respect of whom the order was made and the police have the right to be heard by the court (*subsection (3)*). In relation to the imposition of any additional prohibitions, the court must apply the same test as that which applied when making the order (*subsection (4)*). An order may not be discharged within two years of it being made without the consent of the relevant chief officer of police (*subsection (6)*).

Clause 25: Interim Slavery and Trafficking Risk Orders

70. *Subsections (1) and (2)* provide for an interim STRO to made where an application has been made for an STRO and the court considers that it is just to do so (*subsection (3)*). For example, the court may make an interim order in a case where it is satisfied that this is necessary for the purpose of protecting a person from immediate harm pending the full determination of the application for the order.

71. An interim order must be made for a specified period and ceases to have effect once the main application has been determined (*subsection (4)*). An interim order may be varied, renewed or discharged (*subsection (5)*).

Clause 26: Appeals

72. A person may appeal against the making of a STRO or an interim STRO, or the decision under clause 24 to vary, renew or discharge an order to the Crown Court (*subsection (1)*).

73. *Subsection (2)* sets out the powers of the Crown Court when determining an appeal. It will be open to the court to revoke the order or to amend its provision (either the duration or the prohibitions contained in it).

74. The effect of *subsection (3)* is that any application to vary, renew or discharge an interim STRO made by the Crown Court on appeal must be made to the magistrates' court.

Clause 27: Offences

75. *Subsection (1)* makes it an offence for a person to do anything which is prohibited by a STRO or interim STRO without reasonable excuse.

76. Where an order includes a foreign travel prohibition in respect of all countries outside the United Kingdom, *subsection (2)* makes it an offence for the person subject to the order to fail, without reasonable excuse, to surrender all his or her passports.

77. The maximum penalty for either offence is six months imprisonment or a fine of £5,000 or both on summary conviction, or five years imprisonment following conviction on indictment (*subsection (3)*). *Subsection (4)* precludes the court from making an order for a conditional discharge following a conviction for an offence in this clause.

Clause 28: Guidance

78. This clause confers a duty on the Secretary of State to issue guidance to chief officers and the Director General of the NCA in relation to their powers to apply for STROs and interim STPOs (*subsection (1)*). The Secretary of State may issue revised guidance (*subsection (2)*). The Secretary of State is required to publish such guidance (*subsection (3)*); it is not subject to any parliamentary procedure.

Clause 29: Interpretation of Part 2

79. This clause defines terms used in Part 2 of the Bill.

80. *Subsection (8)* disapplies the usual six month time limit for hearing an application made by complaint to the magistrates' court.

Part 3: The Anti-slavery Commissioner

Clause 30: The Anti-Slavery Commissioner

81. *Subsection (1)* provides for the establishment of an Anti-slavery Commissioner ("the Commissioner") who will be an independent office holder appointed by the Secretary of State (in practice, the Home Secretary)). The duration of an appointment and provision for resignation and removal from office will be provided for in the terms of appointment (*subsection (2)*). *Subsection (3)* makes provision for the payment of expenses, remuneration or allowances. The Commissioner will not be a corporation sole able to employ staff or enter into contracts and, as such, staffing and accommodation will be provided by the Secretary of State after consultation with the Commissioner (*subsection (4)*). *Subsection (5)* has the effect of disqualifying the Commissioner from also being a Member of Parliament and *subsection (6)* makes the Commissioner subject to the provisions of the Freedom of Information Act 2000.

Clause 31: General Functions of Commissioner

82. *Subsection (1)* states that the Commissioner must encourage good practice in the prevention, detection, investigation and prosecution of offences set out in Part 1. In practice the Commissioner will therefore focus on the effectiveness of the law enforcement response in England and Wales to encourage effective investigations leading to successful convictions of modern slavery cases.

83. *Subsection (2)* sets out a non-exhaustive list of things the Commissioner may do in exercise of his/ her general functions in subsection (1). In carrying out his general function the Commissioner may make reports to the Secretary of State on any matter which the Secretary of State has authorised the Commissioner to report on or which the current annual plan states is a matter the Commissioner will report on (see *subsections (2)(a) and (3)*). The Commissioner will report on an annual basis based on the annual plan they agree with the Secretary of State. The Commissioner could also report at other times, for example if they are undertaking a specific programme of work on a particular topic. The Commissioner may make recommendations to public authorities about the exercise of their functions in England and Wales. The Commissioner may undertake research and may support others to do so. This could be administrative support or financial support, where funds are available. The Commissioner may also provide information, education or training to any person, for example to law enforcement agencies on good

practice in investigating modern slavery offences. The Commissioner may also consult any person they feel is appropriate in carrying out their functions.

84. *Subsection (5)* sets out a power for the Secretary of State to remove from any report information that they think should not be included on the grounds of national security, individual safety or prejudice a criminal investigation or prosecution.

85. *Subsection (6)* defines the term "public authority" for the purposes of this clause. One effect of the definition is that an authority will be a "public authority" for the purposes of the clause only if, amongst other things, it exercises functions in England and Wales.

Clause 32: Annual Plans and Annual Reports

86. *Subsection (1)* requires the Commissioner to prepare an annual plan of their programme of work and priorities for the coming year, for approval by the Secretary of State.

87. *Subsection (2)* states that the Commissioner must set out in the annual plan what their objectives and priorities are for the year. In the plan they will also need to include information about any other activities they proposed to undertake in the course of their duties including the matters on which they intend to report under clause 31(2)(a).

88. *Subsection (3)* allows the Secretary of State to approve the annual plan, either without modifications or with modifications agreed with the Commissioner. In practice the Commissioner will work collaboratively with the Secretary of State to produce a mutually agreed plan which focuses on priority areas.

89. *Subsection (4)* requires the Commissioner to provide a report on the activities they have undertaken to fulfil their functions as soon as is reasonably practicable after the end of each calendar year.

90. *Subsection (5)* provides that in producing an annual report the Commissioner must include an assessment of the extent to which they have met the objectives and priorities they set out in their annual plan. The Commissioner must also include a statement of the matters on which the Commissioner has reported under clause 31(2)(a) and a statement of the other activities they have undertaken in the year in carrying out their functions.

91. *Subsection (6)* requires the Secretary of State to lay any annual plan they approve and any annual report they receive from the Commissioner before Parliament.

92. *Subsection (7)* gives the Secretary of State the power to remove information from the annual report before it is laid before Parliament. The

removal of information will be where the Secretary of State thinks that there may be issues of national security, including the information might jeopardise an individual's safety or might prejudice a criminal investigation or prosecution.

Clause 33: Duty to Co-Operate with the Commissioner

93. *Subsection (1)* provides that the Commissioner may request co-operation from a specified public authority where the Commissioner considers that the co-operation is necessary for the purposes of the Commissioner's functions.

94. Subsection (2) provides that a specified public authority, where it is reasonably practicable to do so, must comply with any request for co-operation made to it by the Commissioner.

95. *Subsection (3)* and *subsection (4)* clarifies that information disclosed by an authority to the Commissioner pursuant to subsection (2) will not breach any obligation of confidence owed by the public authority making the disclosure, or any other restriction on the disclosure of information, other than the restrictions found in the Data Protection Act 1998, or Part 1 of the Regulation of Investigatory Powers Act 2000.

96. *Subsection (5)* confirms that "public authority" has the same meaning as in clause 31; and that a "specified public authority" means a public authority which is specified in an order made by the Secretary of State for the purposes of this clause.

Clause 34: Restriction on Exercise of Functions

97. This clause restricts the Commissioner from exercising their functions in relation to particular individuals or cases.

Part 4: Miscellaneous

Clause 35: Duty to Notify NCA About Suspected Victims of Human Trafficking

98. *Subsection (1)* places a duty on public authorities specified in an order (subject to the negative resolution procedure) made by the Secretary of State to notify the NCA where they have reasonable grounds to suspect that a person may be a victim of human trafficking (as defined in *subsection (5)*). It is envisaged that the specified public authorities will include police forces and local authorities. This duty will be different from the existing non-statutory National Referral Mechanism ("NRM").

99. The NRM is a system for children and consenting adults to have their cases assessed by two Competent Authorities within the UK (within the NCA and the Home Office). Individuals can also gain access to support and accommodation once they have received a positive 'reasonable grounds' assessment from a Competent Authority. Further advice regarding the NRM process is available on the NCA website[13]. Currently this is the key source of data on trafficking victims in the UK, but many cases are not reported. In 2012, 1,186 individuals were referred to the NRM, but a further 1,477 were identified through the UK Human Trafficking Centre's 2012 Strategic Assessment. This new duty to report will mean that adult potential victims of trafficking, who do not wish to be referred, assessed and supported through the NRM process will still be referred through for data purposes by specified public authorities.

100. *Subsection (2)* enables the Secretary of State by order (subject to the negative resolution procedure) to prescribe the information that must be included in a notification under subsection (1). It is envisaged that such information will include the nationality of the victim, type of exploitation experienced and the location and dates it took place. Any such order cannot require the disclosure of information in contravention of the Data Protection Act 1998.

101. The Secretary of State may also issue guidance to specified public authorities as to the factors that indicate that a person may be the victim of human trafficking (*subsection (4)*). There is a range of guidance already available to specified public authorities and wider frontline workers who may encounter potential victims of trafficking[14].

Clauses 36 to 40: Final Provisions

102. *Clauses 36 to 40* contain general provisions. Clause 36 allows the Secretary of State by order to make saving, transitional or transitory provision, as well as consequential amendments. The draft Bill does not include a Schedule of consequential amendments. However, it is recognised that, in particular, Part 1 requires many consequential amendments that will be worked up in the coming months. Clause 37 concerns the parliamentary procedure to be adopted for the order making powers under the Bill. Clause 38 limits the extent of the Bill to England and Wales. As indicated, discussions continue on whether that should be extended to cover all the UK. Clause 39 deals with commencement.

Commencement

103. *Clause 39* provides that Clauses 36 to 40 of the draft Bill come into force on Royal Assent. All other provisions of the Bill will be brought into force by means of commencement orders made by the Secretary of State.

Financial Effects of the Bill

The main financial implications of the draft Bill for the public sector lie in the following areas. The figures set out in the paragraphs below are based on a number of assumptions about implementation which are subject to change. Further details of the costs and benefits of the provisions in the draft Bill are set out in the impact assessment published alongside the draft Bill.

104. There are implications for specified public authorities who will be required to report potential victims of trafficking, and the NCA who receive the information. The low volume of reports anticipated (c. 1500 additional per year) is estimated to create an annual cost of around £37,000 per annum.

105. *There will also be costs linked to increased sentences and the management and breach of the new Slavery and Trafficking Prevention Orders and Slavery and Trafficking Risk Orders. We anticipate that these measures will be used against a targeted, relatively small group of defendants and offenders. Each additional year served by an offender will cost the Criminal Justice System around £28,000. If an offender who breaches either the slavery and trafficking prevention order or slavery and trafficking risk order is sentenced in the Crown Court to the maximum custodial penalty, each case could cost up to around £86,000 across the Criminal Justice System*[15].

106. We also estimate the annual cost of the Commissioner, their support staff and activities would be around £300,000-£500,000 per annum.

107. The other provisions in the draft Bill are not expected to have a material financial impact on public sector bodies.

Effects of the Bill on Public Sector Manpower

108. Part 3 of the draft Bill provides for the appointment of an Anti-slavery Commissioner. The Commissioner is expected to be supported by 3 staff from within the Home Office. The other provisions in the draft Bill are not expected to have an impact on public sector manpower.

Summary of Impact Assessments

109. The draft Bill is accompanied by an impact assessment which has been published alongside this draft Bill. The provisions in the draft Bill impact mainly on criminal justice agencies, in particular the police and National

Crime Agency. In addition, clause 35 introduces a duty on specified public authorities to notify the NCA about suspected victims of human trafficking; it is envisaged that the list of specified authorities will include the police, local authorities, border force officers and immigration officers. The Impact Assessment focuses on this measure given its broader impact. Further Impact Assessments will be completed as required prior to introduction of the Bill.

End Notes

[1] Summary of ILO report June 2012: http://www.ilo.org/global/about-the-ilo/newsroom/news/WCMS_181961/lang--en/index.htm.

[2] The National Referral Mechanism (NRM) is an identification and support process for potential victims of modern slavery. It was designed to make it easier for all the different agencies that could be involved in a trafficking case, such as the police, UK Visas and Immigration, local authorities, and designated NGOs to share information about potential victims and to facilitate their access to tailored support.

[3] The phrase ‘potential victims’ is used in relation to the NRM and statistics as it designates that an individual has been referred but not the outcome of that decision which may or may not confirm their victim status.

[4] Second report of the Inter-Departmental Ministerial Group on Human Trafficking: https://www.gov.uk/Government/publications/human-trafficking-inter-departmental-ministerial-group-report-2013.

[5] The SOCA/UKHTC Intelligence Assessment: http://www.nationalcrimeagency.gov.uk/news/publications/15-ukhtc-strategic-assesssment-on-human-traffickingin-2012/file6 Assessment made on the number of positive and outstanding NRM decisions plus intelligence.

[7] https://www.gov.uk/government/uploads/system/uploads/attachment data/file/251487/9794-TSOHMG Human Trafficking.pdf.

[8] Authorised Professional Practice (APP) is the body of consolidated guidance for policing. APP significantly reduces the amount of national guidance in circulation and encourages the use of professional discretion.

[9] https://www.gov.uk/government/publications/serious-organised-crime-strategy.

[10] https://www.gov.uk/government/publications/human-trafficking-inter-departmental-ministerial-group-report-2013.

[11] https://www.gov.uk/government/news/home-secretary-begins-evidence-sessions-on-modern-slavery.

[12] For example, see the orders available under the Sexual Offence Act 2003 (where the victims suffer sexual harm) or the Serious Crime Act 2007.

[13] http://www.nationalcrimeagency.gov.uk/about-us/what-we-do/specialist-capabilities/uk-human-t raffickingcentre/national-referral-mechanism.

[14] https://www.gov.uk/government/policies/reducing-and-preventing-crime--2/supporting-pages/human-trafficking.

[15] *This is an initial estimate and is subject to change as cost estimates are refined.*

In: Human Trafficking
Editor: Mildred Sapienti

ISBN: 978-1-63117-675-3

Chapter 4

HUMAN TRAFFICKING: THE GOVERNMENT'S STRATEGY*

Her Majesty's Government

FOREWORD BY THE HOME SECRETARY

Human trafficking destroys lives and its effects damage communities. The transport and exploitation of vulnerable men, women and children by predatory organised criminal groups is something that no civilised country should tolerate. We need to do more to stop this horrific crime.

The UK has a good record in tackling human trafficking. That is something we must build on. Our new strategy for tackling human trafficking has four key aims: international action to stop trafficking happening in the first place; a stronger border at home to stop victims being brought into the UK; tougher law enforcement action to tackle the criminal gangs that orchestrate the crime; and improved identification and care for the victims of trafficking.

Human trafficking is a truly international crime, with potential victims identified from over 80 different countries to date. We are determined to work more closely with our international partners in transit and source countries to stop this terrible crime. By applying to opt in to the EU Directive on human trafficking, we have demonstrated our commitment to working with other

* This is an edited, reformatted and augmented version of a policy paper, dated July 2011. This paper contains public sector information licensed under the Open Government Licence v2.0 (United Kingdom).

countries in Europe to drive up standards across the continent in tackling trafficking. This is particularly important as we head towards the Olympics and Paralympics in 2012. Monitoring intelligence will help us to respond quickly and appropriately to any potential increased risk of trafficking.

After being taken from a source country and transiting third countries, victims of trafficking must then cross the UK border. For too long our response at the border has not been well enough informed or coordinated. Fulfilling a key pledge in the Programme for Government, in June I announced that we would establish a new National Crime Agency (NCA) containing a dedicated Border Policing Command to strengthen our borders and help prevent human trafficking and other serious crimes.

A further aspect of preventing trafficking is to take tough action against the organised criminals who run the abhorrent trade in human beings. Again, the NCA will have a key role by using its enhanced intelligence capabilities and its coordination and tasking functions to target the organised criminal groups involved in human trafficking.

As well as increasing prevention, we are also committed to further improving the level of support for victims. Victims of trafficking have been deceived and exploited. They will undoubtedly be frightened and vulnerable. We must therefore do all we can to support them as they try to rebuild their lives. Recognising the importance of this area, we have protected the level of funding at £2 million per year for the next two years, even at a time when savings have to be made across Government.

The National Referral Mechanism provides a way for all agencies such as the police, the UK Border Agency, local authorities and Non-Governmental Organisations to cooperate, share information about potential victims, identify those victims and facilitate their access to advice, accommodation and support. We are making the National Referral Mechanism more accessible and I am delighted that the NSPCC and Barnardo's have recently joined and are now able to help child victims of trafficking to get the help they need.

The Government's commitment to tackling human trafficking is clear and unequivocal. Our strategy will give a renewed focus on prevention overseas, a stronger border at home, tougher action on the perpetrators and better identification and care for the victims. These measures will make a real difference to the lives of those at risk of human trafficking.

Theresa May
Home Secretary

SECTION 1. BACKGROUND ON TRAFFICKING

1. Human trafficking is international organised crime, with the exploitation of human beings for profit at its heart. It is an abuse of basic rights, with organised criminals preying on vulnerable people to make money. In most cases, victims are brought to the UK from abroad, but we know that trafficking also occurs within the UK and that children in particular are increasingly vulnerable to falling victim to exploitation.

2. The United Nations Convention against Transnational Organised Crime (the 'Palermo Protocol') describes trafficking as:

> "the recruitment, transportation, transfer, harbouring or receipt of persons, by means of the threat or use of force or other forms of coercion, of abduction, of fraud, of deception, of the abuse of power or of a position of vulnerability or of the giving or receiving of payments or benefits to achieve the consent of a person having control over another person, for the purpose of exploitation.

Exploitation shall include, at a minimum, the exploitation of the prostitution of others or other forms of sexual exploitation, forced labour or services, slavery or practices similar to slavery, servitude or the removal of organs[1]."

3. Historically, most adult victims identified were women trafficked for sexual exploitation. However, recent trends suggest that trafficking for labour exploitation could become more prevalent than other forms of trafficking.

4. Child trafficking victims are brought to the UK for many purposes, including sexual exploitation, domestic servitude, benefit fraud, cannabis farming, street begging, theft and shoplifting.

5. The greatest numbers of adult victims come to the UK from China, South East Asia, and Eastern Europe; child victims are trafficked in the greatest numbers from Vietnam, Nigeria, China and Eastern Europe. However, this is a truly international crime, with potential victims from over 80 different countries referred to the National Referral Mechanism (NRM) since its inception and 47 different counties identified as sources of child trafficking to the UK by CEOP[2].

6. The hidden nature of trafficking makes it difficult to gain an accurate picture of its true scale and nature. Recent evidence has started to build a clearer picture of the numbers of victims in the UK. Project Acumen[3], a study by the Association of Chief Police Officers (ACPO) estimates that there are at

least 2,600 female adult victims of trafficking for sexual exploitation in England and Wales. Reports from the Child Exploitation and Online Protection Centre suggest there are on average around 300 child trafficking victims in the UK per annum[4] with 322 potential child victims referred to the NRM between 1 April 2009 and 31 December 2010. In contrast the UK's human trafficking victim identification and support framework, the National Referral Mechanism (NRM), recorded 1,254 potential victims of trafficking in the UK referred from 1 April 2009 to 31 December 2010, broken down as follows:

Exploitation Type	Number of referrals Child	Adult
Sexual Exploitation	99	438
Labour Exploitation	98	267
Domestic Servitude	44	175
Unspecified Exploitation	81	52
Totals	322	932
No of Prosecutions - 2010/11	116*	

* Number of prosecutions recorded by the Crown Prosecution Service.

7. Victims may travel to the UK willingly, in the belief that they are destined for a better life, including paid work and may start their journey believing they are economic migrants, either legally or illegally. They may also believe that the people arranging their passage and papers are merely facilitators, helping with their journey, rather than people who aim to exploit them. In other cases, victims may start their journey independently and come to rely on facilitators along different stages of their journey to arrange papers and transportation.

8. The ease of international travel has led to the opportunity for increased movement of people across borders, both legally and illegally, especially from poorer to wealthier countries such as the UK. This has created opportunities for traffickers who use poverty, war, crisis and ignorance to lure vulnerable migrants to the UK for exploitation.

9. Traffickers use threats, force, coercion, abduction, fraud, deception, abuse of power and payment to control their victim. And most traffickers are organised criminals. It is estimated that 17% of organised criminal networks operating in the UK are involved in organised immigration crime, of which a small proportion is human trafficking[5]. Some groups organise the trafficking process from beginning to end, while others sub-contract aspects of the process, such as money laundering, or obtaining illegal passports and visas.

10. Offenders are primarily driven by profit. The UK Threat Assessment judges that 'organised immigration crime is lucrative enough to attract and maintain the interest of organised criminals'[6]. Trafficking offers opportunity for profit because the continual exploitation of the victim's body or labour generates money over a period of time. Underpinning this profit is demand, with people living in the UK paying money for sex or the products of labour exploitation.

11. Government strategy builds on the UK's record on human trafficking and forms part of the Government's wider strategy on violence against women and girls. It recognises the good work already under way, particularly on victim care and sets out how we will strengthen our efforts to prevent people from becoming trafficking victims in the first place.

SECTION 2. OUR RESPONSE TO COMBATING HUMAN TRAFFICKING

AIM: To tackle trafficking from end to end: from recruitment to exploitation, ensuring agencies have the right tools and intelligence to reduce the threat, and maintaining effective victim support.

12. Traffickers have significant profit at stake and run businesses in order to maintain it. Our response needs to be as dynamic and agile as the traffickers to be able to stay one step ahead of them. And our response needs to reach across organisational and national boundaries.

13. Our strategy focuses on four key areas:

- Improved victim care arrangements
- Enhanced ability to act early, before the harm has reached the UK
- Smarter multi-agency action at the border
- Better coordination of our law enforcement efforts within the UK

14. In developing this strategy we have considered the differing needs of victims whether they are men, women, or children. Section 7 focuses particularly on child victims as we recognise the significant harm caused to children who are victims of exploitation.

15. Raising the risks to the traffickers and going after their profits must be at the heart of our approach to drive them out of this business and to stop more

vulnerable men, women and children becoming trafficking victims. In particular, this means a greater emphasis on disruption and enforcement activity.

16. While all human trafficking is abhorrent, the Government notes the particularly vulnerable position of children trafficked to and within the UK. We are determined to do all we can to prevent and safeguard children from the threat of child traffickers and to ensure that, where child victims are identified, they receive the best support and protection the UK can provide.

17. The National Crime Agency (NCA), on its establishment in 2013, will build on and enhance the UK's capabilities. It will connect the efforts of local policing and neighbourhood action to national agencies and action overseas to improve the UK's response to serious and organised crime, including human trafficking, and strengthen arrangements at the border. The NCA will comprise distinct command units for Organised Crime, Border Policing, Economic Crime, and the Child Exploitation and Online Protection Centre (CEOP), and will build on the capabilities and expertise of its precursor organisations such as SOCA, which includes the UK Human Trafficking Centre (UKHTC). At its heart will be an intelligence hub which will build and maintain a comprehensive picture of the threats, harms and risks to the UK from organised crime. Building on the existing, improved capability of the UKHTC, this hub will draw in intelligence from a wide range of law enforcement organisations – such as the police and UK Border Agency – to form a comprehensive picture of organised crime that the UKHTC will be able to use in tackling those involved in human trafficking.

A Shared Responsibility

18. We recognise, in the fight against traffickers, continued coordination and collaboration across the UK is vital. We will continue the close and regular communication between HM Government and the Devolved Administrations, driven by the biannual UK-wide Inter-Departmental Ministerial Group.

19. Government and law enforcement agencies cannot tackle human trafficking alone. The voluntary sector, through its expertise and its commitment to dealing with the effects of trafficking is a vital partner. The private sector also has a role to play. Traffickers and their enablers exploit legitimate businesses in order to run their trade. Businesses have an important role to play in raising the risks to traffickers and making it more difficult for

them to exploit victims. We will therefore work with the private sector to strengthen our overall approach to tackling trafficking to ensure business remains aware of its social duty in reporting suspected incidences of trafficking.

20. Many members of the public already care deeply about the plight of trafficking victims and about the impact it has on their communities. We will explore what further role the public can play in identifying information about trafficking and how we can raise awareness and vigilance in particular communities. We will also monitor intelligence in the run up to the Olympics and Paralympics in 2012 to ensure we are alerted early to any potential increase in trafficking.

SECTION 3. IMPROVED VICTIM IDENTIFICATION AND CARE

AIM: To identify victims of trafficking and provide support tailored to the victim's needs.

We will do this by improving the National Referral Mechanism and implementing a more flexible contracting model in England and Wales to identify and support victims.

21. Victims of trafficking are some of the hardest to reach and most vulnerable victims. Hidden away, deceived, exploited and frightened – they need to be formally identified and provided with a tailored response that fits their vulnerability and helps us to bring their abusers to justice.

22. The UK already has a good record in this area and we want to build on that.

Our International Commitments

23. The UK implemented the Council of Europe Convention on Action against Trafficking in Human Beings in 2009, signing up to a set of minimum standards on the identification, protection and support of trafficking victims, including:

- the granting of a recovery and reflection period for identified victims, during which removal action is halted. The UK grants a minimum 45-day period – this is 15 days more than the 30-day minimum standard.
- the issuing of residence permits for conclusively identified victims in certain circumstances. The UK grants a minimum period of 1 year.

24. A key part of the support package under the Convention is the National Referral Mechanism (NRM). This helps in determining whether someone is a victim of trafficking so that they can have access to support, such as accommodation, medical care, training and education, translation services, as well as psychological and material help. The NRM provides a way for all agencies such as the police, the UK Border Agency, local authorities and Non-Governmental Organisations to cooperate, share information about potential victims and facilitate their access to advice, accommodation and support.

25. The Crown Prosecution Service (CPS), through its public policy statement, is also improving engagement with victims. The policy statement explains to those involved in supporting trafficking victims the criminal justice process as well as what support and protection can be provided to victims who decide to engage with criminal proceedings. We also encourage all organisations and agencies to ensure that officials who are likely to have any contact with the victims of trafficking are provided with awareness training.

26. The Government has also recently announced its intention to opt in to the EU Directive on Human Trafficking, subject to acceptance by the European Commission. This further demonstrates the UK's commitment to tackling human trafficking and providing support to victims. We will work with key partners both within the UK and the EU to implement the Directive effectively by April 2013.

Ensuring Victims Get the Protection They Deserve

27. We want to build on these foundations and improve how the National Referral Mechanism (NRM) works. We will raise the quality of decision-making by running case review exercises and auditing decisions. Feedback to staff will enhance the quality of decisions, identify trends and point the way for further improvement.

Identifying victims under the NRM

Under the NRM, frontline staff from designated agencies and organisations who find themselves with grounds for concern that a person may be a victim of human trafficking make a referral to the National Referral Mechanism. These are known as First Responders.

Decisions about who is a victim of trafficking are then made by trained specialists in designated 'Competent Authorities'. The UK's Competent Authorities currently sit in the UK Human Trafficking Centre (UKHTC) which is part of the Serious Organised Crime Agency (SOCA), and the UK Border Agency.

28. We are making the NRM more accessible by enabling more organisations to refer victims to it. The NSPCC - Child Trafficking Advice and Information Line and Barnardo's have recently joined and are now able to refer child victims into the system.

29. The Department of Health (DH) will work with the UKHTC and others, to improve the response from health services to victims of trafficking. This will include equipping more health services and professionals with the training and skills to become first responders. DH is working with the Women's Health and Equality Consortium on the trafficking and health project to agree specific actions to promote greater awareness of human trafficking and provide health professionals with guidance on how to respond to victims appropriately. The Department of Health has also recognised the need for better understanding of the issues around health and trafficking and has therefore invited bids for a piece of research in this area which is due to commence in 2011.

30. Identifying trafficking victims relies on agencies and the public knowing what signs to look for. We will raise awareness of trafficking among frontline staff through:

- implementation of the findings of the trafficking and health project – to promote training and awareness of health professionals; and
- working with the London Safeguarding Children Board to raise awareness amongst local authorities through their Child Trafficking Toolkit.

31. We will also improve:

- how our immigration system handles potential victims of trafficking and ensure the UK Border Agency's Asylum Screening Unit (ASU) officers are trained in identifying vulnerable applicants so there is greater gender sensitivity;
- the information supplied to asylum seekers when they first apply for asylum and the information available on the UK Border Agency website to provide assurances around dealing sensitively with claims and what to expect of the asylum process;
- the identification and treatment of vulnerable people in the asylum system, so that it is more sensitive to the individual's needs or circumstances.

32. All NRM decisions are reviewed by a second decision-maker who is not involved in any asylum or immigration decision relating to the potential victim of trafficking. We have already made a number of improvements to victim identification, including the training and guidance available to decision-makers. We will continue to look for ways to enhance victim identification decision-making through driving up the quality of decisions and exploring the best match with immigration decision-making systems.

Improving the Care of Victims

33. Victim care is central to our approach to combating trafficking through providing identified trafficking victims with the proper support they need and deserve. That is why we have protected the funding for supporting adult victims of trafficking at £2 million per year in England and Wales.

34. Significant improvements have been made to the support of victims of human trafficking in recent years, with a greater understanding of the needs of victims and an increase in the number of organisations supporting them.

35. However, we want the best possible services to be provided to the largest number of victims within the resources available. The previous Government channelled support to victims through a small number of voluntary-sector organisations. We want to see a more diverse sector, where a range of support is on offer and innovation is encouraged.

36. We have therefore introduced a new model for funding adult support in England and Wales from 1 July 2011. The Salvation Army will be the

central contractor who will have a case-management function as well as responsibility for overseeing and coordinating the provision of care. Under this model, funding will follow the victim to whichever organisation supports them, allowing the support system to adapt to changing demand and develop a greater range of service provision.

37. This flexibility will provide a tailored service to victims, taking account of their individual needs. This will also make it easier to track a victim through the system and monitor the quality of the service provided. To ensure appropriate victim care is maintained, the Home Office will monitor delivery of the new funding model in conjunction with the Ministry of Justice on a quarterly basis.

38. Whilst we already have comprehensive arrangements in place for trafficked children we are committed to improving identification and the safeguarding response for those who fall victim to this terrible crime. We will raise awareness of this crime and better equip practitioners to identify and safeguard child victims through updated guidance. By working with the CPS we will ensure that children are not unnecessarily criminalised and work with partners to reduce instances of children going missing. The totality of this approach will allow better and earlier identification and ensure tailored support to each individual child.

SECTION 4. ENHANCING OUR ABILITY TO ACT EARLY

AIM: To deter and disrupt trafficking overseas and make the UK a less attractive target for criminals. We will do this by sharing intelligence across boundaries, targeting traffickers before they reach the UK, and communicating the risks to potential victims.

39. Disrupting criminal networks abroad stops the problem before it reaches our borders and stops people becoming victims of trafficking in the first place. This needs to be underpinned with greater awareness-raising in source countries to reduce the supply of potential victims.

40. We will work closely with our international partners to improve the enforcement and awareness-raising response; we will work with overseas governments, international law enforcement agencies such as INTERPOL, Europol and Frontex, and local law enforcement in source countries.

41. This strategy builds on the good work already under way in source countries, and the strong relationships in place between the UK and our

international partners. We have developed country-specific expertise from years of working in source countries and building relationships with local agencies. However, there is more to do to stop the problem before it reaches the UK and raise the importance of the issue abroad. We will therefore explore greater opportunities to work with other countries – by focusing on targeting traffickers before they reach the UK and preventing more people from becoming victims in the first place.

42. The NCA, once established, will bring even greater focus to this work, putting its full weight behind representing the UK's interests internationally. It will work with international law enforcement partners and UK partners, such as the UK Border Agency, Foreign and Commonwealth Office and the Department for International Development, to prevent the importation of serious and organised criminality into this country. It will work with international partners to tackle and disrupt criminals, such as human traffickers, who target the UK from overseas.

The UK's Overseas Agencies Working to a Common Purpose

43. To better coordinate and direct our work overseas, we will give the UK Human Trafficking Centre responsibility for collating and analysing information on trafficking to inform our strategic approach and drive our operational response. This will ensure the right information is disseminated to the operational frontline. We will work with other agencies to ensure that the information that we gather is as consistent and thorough as possible, and is fed consistently into our Organised Crime Mapping tools.

44. We will use the cross-government Country Business Plans (CBPs) to ensure that the priorities and objectives of all departments and agencies are aligned and clear across government. This will mean that, where a trafficking issue has been identified in a country, Ambassadors and High Commissioners will ensure that appropriate local action is taken. The plans will help us to tailor our activity to the country in question, including ways of working with local law enforcement agencies to address specific risks and threats.

45. The CPS also plays an important role in preventing harm from reaching the UK. Using its prosecutors' training package the CPS is working with source countries to improve the ability of overseas investigators and prosecutors in case building and prosecution. To improve the criminal justice framework for trafficking, the CPS works with authorities in source countries to improve international cooperation and to facilitate prosecutor placements in

key countries. The CPS is also working with UK investigators and prosecutors to improve the provision of information and evidence to support prosecutions in the UK.

46. The establishment of the NCA in 2013 will make further improvements possible, with its Border Policing Command aiming to prevent threats reaching UK shores where possible. Informed by a single national threat assessment and strategy, the NCA's Border Policing Command will ensure that all law enforcement agencies operating in and around the border work to clear, mutually-agreed priorities to strengthen our border and address national security threats. A unified intelligence picture will drive the authority of the NCA to task and coordinate resources across law enforcement to tackle serious and organised criminality, including human trafficking. Building on SOCA's existing capability, the crime-fighting reach of the NCA will extend UK-wide and overseas, recognising and respecting the primacy of those in whose territories it operates.

Focusing on Priority Countries

47. We will improve our overseas work on trafficking by ensuring that evidence drives our priorities and operational response. Information from victims and de-briefs will ensure our strategic and operational response is up to date.

48. Evidence suggests that some countries top the list repeatedly as areas of concern for trafficking. We will therefore focus on those transit and source countries from where the greatest threat originates, through the Country Business Plans.

Diplomatic Engagement

49. Diplomatic engagement can help the work of UK officials in encouraging and brokering disruption activity against traffickers. While we have excellent diplomatic relationships with many of the key countries, we are working to overcome the barriers that might remain, such as some countries not considering trafficking as a priority, and therefore being reluctant to engage in disruption activity.

50. We will use the Country Business Plans to make delivery agencies on the ground and up to Ambassador-level aware of the important role they can

play in contributing to an effective, Government-wide effort to tackle human trafficking. Through closer working we will engage with foreign governments to ensure that common challenges are identified, and that they work with us to address those challenges through, for example, capacity building.

Workshop for Chinese consular and immigration officials

In 2010 UK Border Agency officials supported a two-day workshop in Beijing organised by the International Organization for Migration (IOM) for senior Chinese consular and immigration officials to strengthen victim identification procedures and introduce safe and voluntary repatriation mechanisms for victims of human trafficking. We will continue to work with other countries to ensure their staff have the tools necessary to lead the fight on trafficking.

Increasing Our Ability to Disrupt Overseas

Intelligence Sharing

51. Better intelligence gathering and sharing is central to the disruption of trafficking. Law enforcement agencies in the UK hold valuable intelligence which, when collated centrally by the UKHTC, will deliver a better threat assessment, and enable us to identify traffickers before they traffick victims into the UK. This will be further enhanced through the creation of the NCA's central intelligence hub.

52. In order to intervene overseas, we need to increase our understanding of how and why people become victims of trafficking. De-briefing victims and traffickers is key to building this intelligence. De-briefing is already carried out by many agencies, but can reflect a specific agency's priorities and not take account of the wider picture. More standardisation of de-briefing practices will ensure that opportunities are not missed.

53. We will, therefore, ensure de-briefing is set up in such a way that when one agency carries out a de-brief, they are gathering the information needed by all agencies – from recruitment, to transit route, to how they crossed the UK border, to activity within the UK. Information collated will be passed to UKHTC, as the central repository of data on trafficking, analysed, and used to inform relevant posts upstream.

Joint Operational Work

54. To stop trafficking before it reaches the UK, we need to work with those law enforcement agencies in priority countries that are able to prosecute the criminals acting within their jurisdiction. SOCA (and, from 2013, the National Crime Agency), and the UK Border Agency will work together on operational activity in order to include a greater focus on referring tactical intelligence on trafficking to local law enforcement.

55. Building on this disruption activity, we will work increasingly closely with the airline industry to enhance its knowledge of human trafficking and provide its staff with the tools needed to identify victims of trafficking and trigger an intervention. This will include developing training for carriers and their staff that raises awareness of the behavioural indicators associated with trafficking.

RALON

The UK Border Agency's Risk and Liaison Overseas Network (RALON) operates in more than 50 locations worldwide to identify and reduce the threats to the UK border.

RALON officers work with airlines and local border control authorities to ensure passengers hold the right travel documents before they travel to the UK. In 2010 they prevented over 67,000 people with incorrect, counterfeit or fraudulently obtained travel documents from travelling to the UK. RALON officers have trained carriers on routes that are commonly used by traffickers to enable them to identify traffickers and their victims.

Example of RALON's work against trafficking

The UK Border Agency identified a trend of Nigerian adults and children arriving at UK airports destined for the vice industry in Europe. The RALON officer in Paris noted the profile and was able to intervene with six victims who were referred to local law enforcement for care. The officer used this profile to identify one of the suspected traffickers and working with her partners in the French Border Police not only prevented him from reaching the UK, but facilitated his removal from France to Nigeria.

Educating Potential Victims

We are already working to educate potential victims in source countries about the dangers of trafficking. In China and Thailand there has been significant work on trafficking awareness and prevention with the International Organization for Migration, United Nations Office on Drugs and Crime (UNODC) and other organisations. In Malawi, the Salvation Army has run a project to improve knowledge of and access to rights for children who have been trafficked or are vulnerable to being trafficked. But many potential victims do not know they are at risk of exploitation until it is too late, and some may ignore the warnings. We will continue to work with source countries to raise awareness among those who may be at risk of becoming a trafficking victim.

Sharing Information and Resources with Other Destination Countries

57. Alerting people to the risks associated with smuggling services is not a problem facing the UK alone. Through the Five Country Conference (FCC), the UK works with the United States, Canada, Australia and New Zealand on common immigration-related challenges. We will continue to work with our FCC partners to identify best practice in deterring the use of people smugglers and, where possible, will work with our partners on coordinated education projects.

58. We are also committed to working with the EU and the Council of Europe. Practical engagement with Council of Europe and EU Member States will allow us to share intelligence and law enforcement expertise, exchange best practice on investigation and prosecution of traffickers, and share resources.

59. The international sharing of information is well-established, but challenges remain around what is done with the information. The recent EU Directive on human trafficking paves the way for further engagement with EU-wide organisations and governments to share our prosecution and investigation expertise. The UKHTC will send staff members to Member States in order to share UK best practice and contribute to raising the standard of anti-trafficking work.

60. We will also work closely with labour inspectorates across EU Member States to achieve common standards on identifying and punishing labour exploitation.

61. We will explore further the opportunities for establishing joint operations with overseas counterparts, building on the success of Operation Golf, a joint Metropolitan Police Service and Romanian National Police investigation team.

> The Joint Investigation Team set up in September 2008 comprised officers from the Metropolitan Police Service and the Romanian National Police. The action by both police forces led to the identification of 181 trafficked Romanian children and the arrest of 26 suspects in Romania, who were charged with a range of offences including the trafficking of Roma children.

Section 5. Smarter Action at the Border

AIM: To strengthen our border controls and policing to prevent traffickers entering the country

62. A strong border is a key aspect of our strategy. With over 218 million passengers at UK airports in 2009, identifying traffickers and their victims is a challenge. That challenge will increase as the number of passengers is expected to grow to between 410 and 480 million passengers by 2030. The border is no longer a fixed line on a map. By using new technology, particularly biometrics and advance travel information, we are creating an offshore line of defence, able to check individuals at the point of departure and through each stage of their journey.

63. An effective response to trafficking at the border requires a range of statutory and non-statutory agencies to work together to share information and maximise their shared capability. The creation of the UK Border Agency in 2008 improved border security by bringing together customs, immigration and visa staff to form a single organisation. The creation of the National Crime Agency in 2013, with a new Border Policing Command, will further strengthen the response at the border. By doing more with our immigration powers at the border, in the UK and overseas, we can identify traffickers and prevent them from entering the UK.

64. The NCA will play a key role in strengthening the UK border, ensuring that all law enforcement agencies operating in and around the border work to clear and mutually agreed priorities, informed by a shared understanding of the threats and vulnerabilities. The intelligence hub at the heart of the NCA will build and maintain a comprehensive picture of the threats, harms and risks to the UK from organised crime. This will drive the coordination, prioritisation and targeting of action against organised criminals, including those involved in human trafficking.

65. In response to the existing threat of human trafficking we have already taken steps to strengthen the border:

- border staff are trained in child protection issues and human trafficking;
- multi-agency child safeguarding and investigation teams are in place at the UK's major ports;
- overseas border controls have been strengthened by placing officers in France and Belgium to stop illegal immigrants before they get to the UK;
- our ability to fix people's identities by collecting biometrics from all visa applicants has improved;
- and amendments to the Points Based System ensure the right people are allowed to come to the UK.

66. We also use alerts and intelligence to give our officers the information they need to intervene and through the National Border Targeting Centre (NBTC) and Targeting Hubs we will be checking advance passenger information to provide real-time targets to front-line officers.

67. These steps have strengthened our ability to detect and disrupt trafficking, but we need to better understand the risks posed by individuals or groups so that we can target our efforts effectively. e-Borders and other passenger information will also help, but we need better risk indicators and improved coordination between law enforcement partners. Through the National Crime Agency and its Border Policing Command, we will draw on the capability of a wide range of organisations and focus efforts on detection, intervention and the gathering and sharing of intelligence. To lay the groundwork for the NCA, the Organised Crime Coordination Centre will be established within SOCA.

This will develop the national tasking and coordination mechanism. Building on our recent scoping work with Frontex, we are also developing a set of UK specific risk indicators that can be deployed at our ports.

> The European border agency, Frontex, is currently drawing up risk profiles on victims in cooperation with selected Member States, and profiles for traffickers in cooperation with Europol. The risk profiles will be used during border control activities across Europe. They will contribute to more carefully targeted operations against trafficking and identify traffickers and their victims.

68. We will continue to use our visa controls to deny entry to traffickers, preventing them from boarding flights to the UK through the work of the RALON network or refusing them entry at our border. We are committed to ensuring that where potential trafficking victims are identified at the border they are assessed for risk of return.

We will also pass on intelligence about traffickers to overseas law enforcement agencies where we have the legal means to do so.

The Border's Contribution to the Joint Intelligence Picture

69. Better intelligence gathering and sharing will ensure that details of suspected traffickers are available to law enforcement, helping us to prevent known criminals and victims from travelling to the UK. Human trafficking intelligence will be coordinated by the UK Human Trafficking Centre, to increase intelligence flow to and from our UK and overseas posts, with further benefits to come from the NCA intelligence hub from 2013.

70. We will issue further guidance to all frontline border staff so that they understand what information is relevant to human trafficking, how it should be shared, and how to do this quickly so as to support effective intervention. All our law enforcement officers in country, at the border and overseas have the opportunity to shape the intelligence picture as they are likely to come across information that can help us better understand who is involved in trafficking and the methods used.

Disrupting at Visa Application

71. Refusing to issue visas to suspected traffickers and their victims can disrupt trafficking before it reaches the UK. We check visa applicants' fingerprints against a range of police, immigration and security databases before we decide on an application, so as to ensure that foreign nationals with serious criminal histories in the UK are prevented from returning. We will continue to work with law enforcement partners in the UK and overseas to develop and share intelligence on traffickers and their victims to inform our decisions, enabling us to prioritise our checks to target potential criminals and the individuals at greatest risk of being trafficked. We are improving and standardising the way we identify risks, making better use of information and technology to ensure that the best information is available to the officers making decisions on visa applications.

72. The use of false identities and documents as a means to enter the UK illegally is a key enabler for organised crime groups involved in trafficking. We will continue our efforts to identify false documents through the use of forgery detection equipment and through cooperation with overseas agencies to verify the documents we receive. We will continue to deter and disrupt the use of false documentation and identities by working with airlines, strengthening checks on visa applicants, using appropriate biometric information, and working with overseas law enforcement and international partners to share information.

Disrupting at the Border

73. Our aim is to build up as rich an understanding as possible of the routes and methods used by traffickers and to use this information to prevent traffickers, and migrants who are particularly vulnerable to trafficking, from coming to the UK. Staff based at the physical UK border will continue to provide an important line of defence and use immigration powers to prevent high risk individuals from entering the UK. We will ensure our border staff have access to the right information and intelligence to identify and scrutinise those most at risk.

74. We will ensure that intelligence gathered in-country and overseas, including details held by the UKHTC on those convicted or suspected of trafficking is passed to staff at the border. This will help maximise rules-based targeting and ensure individuals linked to trafficking are closely scrutinised at

the border. Our response at the border will also focus on groups who may not be known to UK authorities, but fit a trafficker or vulnerable migrant profile. We will start to use risk-based indicators at the border to facilitate the systematic targeting of high-risk passengers, focusing attention on passengers who pose the highest risk, and allowing the vast majority of legitimate travellers to pass through without delay.

75. We will maximise the use of our e-Borders capability so we are alerted when passengers who are a known risk or those identified through risk-based indicators intend to travel. This will enable us to focus our resources and ensure we scrutinise high risk passengers effectively.

e-Borders is an electronic borders scheme designed to improve the security, efficiency and effectiveness of the border. It will collect and analyse information from carriers (including airlines, ferries and rail companies) about passengers who intend to travel to or from the UK before they travel. This record of passenger movements significantly strengthens the security of the UK by telling us in advance who plans to cross our border so that we can check travellers against lists of people known to pose a threat. It will also enable us to focus staff resources better so that we can stop passengers who are most likely to pose a risk and allow the vast majority of passengers to pass through our border quickly.

e-Borders currently screens more than 55% of all passenger and crew movement and will screen over 90% by the end of this Parliament. Passenger screening is already paying dividends: between April 2005 and January 2011 275 million passenger movements had been checked, resulting in over 7,900 arrests for crimes including murder, rape, assault, and facilitation.

76. In the longer term, the new NCA, and in particular its Border Policing Command will draw on the capability of a wide range of organisations and will deliver a greater number of interventions against trans-national criminal gangs, including those involved in the trafficking of people. The Border Policing Command will coordinate and task operational activity against priorities, using the NCA and other policing and law enforcement agencies' operational resources where appropriate. This will further increase our capability to intervene against trafficking at the border.

Juxtaposed Controls

77. A significant number of trafficking victims enter the UK illegally with false documents or by clandestine entry. This suggests many begin their journey believing they are being smuggled. In response to the threats associated with smuggling and trafficking, a key element of our border control is our offshore presence in northern France and Belgium at the 'juxtaposed controls'. These controls, which are immigration controls performed outside the UK by UK immigration staff, are key to reducing the number of illegal migrants travelling to the UK.

78. The UK Border Agency has resources deployed in ports, at international rail terminals and on board Eurostar services to stop illegal immigrants before they get to the UK; these 'juxtaposed controls' have strengthened the cross-channel border control dramatically. Our officers are now able to stop anyone with false, stolen or inadequate documents, or those who do not qualify for entry to the UK, before they travel. From April 2008 to the end of March 2009 we searched more than a million freight vehicles for illegal immigrants at the juxtaposed controls, and together with our partners prevented over 30,000 individual attempts by people to cross the Channel illegally. We will continue to work with our French partners, as part of the Evian Arrangement, by building on our joint operations and engaging in new initiatives to reinforce the security of our common border, so as to make it more resistant to illegal immigration and trafficking networks.

SECTION 6. MORE COORDINATION OF OUR LAW ENFORCEMENT EFFORTS IN THE UK

AIM: To strengthen our response to traffickers through the creation of the National Crime Agency (NCA)and the Organised Crime Coordination Centre, leading to better identification of organised criminals and a more coordinated response.

79. While strengthening our response overseas and at the border, there must be no let up in our response within the UK. Law enforcement partners already undertake valuable work to tackle trafficking and recent successful convictions, along with continued work to rescue victims, are testament to their efforts. 116 prosecutions for trafficking, and more for related offences,

were secured in 2010/11. High-profile police- led operations have also shown the value of concerted joint working to tackle trafficking.

80. The UKHTC, part of SOCA, is central to these efforts, acting as a repository for intelligence and providing specialist tactical advice to police forces and others undertaking trafficking operations. Its move to SOCA has strengthened its role, by putting it at the heart of our work to tackle organised crime. This is supported by a specialist strategic child trafficking function in the Child Exploitation and Online Protection Centre which provides a child safeguarding perspective on trafficking. At a local level, every police force has an officer specifically trained in human trafficking investigations. The creation of the NCA will strengthen our efforts in this regard.

81. However, we know there is more to do to enhance our in-country enforcement response. The risk to traffickers remains too low, and the profits they can generate are too high and too secure. Only by reversing this, and disrupting their activity, increasing the risk of being convicted, and seizing their criminal profits, will we drive human trafficking out of the UK.

Improved Tasking and Coordination to Disrupt Traffickers

82. Offenders may still perceive trafficking as a 'low risk' crime because of the relatively low risk of being caught (especially in comparison to drugs offences)[7]. We need to improve coordination of our law enforcement response so that we maximise the risk to offenders and maximise the impact of our resources.

83. The establishment of the NCA by 2013, together with the forthcoming Organised Crime Strategy, are significant changes to the national policing landscape and our strengthened response to organised crime.

84. To prepare for this, and as part of the NCA build, the Government will establish the multi-agency Organised Crime Coordination Centre. The centre will be based initially within SOCA and will have a dual reporting line to ACPO. The Centre will lay the foundation for the transition to the NCA by: improving the coordination of our organised crime response; developing the national tasking and coordination mechanism to be led by the National Crime Agency; and developing an improved understanding of the threat from organised crime through the analysis of multiple data and intelligence sources.

85. This will mean that even before the establishment of the NCA, enforcement activity against traffickers will benefit from much greater

coordination. The UK Human Trafficking Centre will be a part of these arrangements while maintaining its specialist functions on trafficking.

Identifying the Criminals

86. Organised Crime Group Mapping will create a multi-agency picture of organised crime threats and targets to inform operational activity against criminals. Held by the Organised Crime Coordination Centre, this index will record offenders involved in trafficking, where they are operating, and will be updated regularly. This will support a dynamic, flexible approach to tackling trafficking, providing a constantly evolving picture of the threats, and allowing activity to be focused on the highest harm.

87. As part of SOCA, the UKHTC has a pivotal role to play in these procedures. It currently collects intelligence from different agencies in the UK. In conjunction with other agencies the UKHTC will collate and analyse intelligence from police forces, UK Border Agency, SOCA, CEOP, and the Gangmaster's Licensing Authority to feed into Organised Crime Group Mapping.

This relationship will be further enhanced by the intelligence hub of the NCA and the close relationships across the new Agency's four commands. The UKHTC will also do more to exploit the intelligence opportunities offered by the National Referral Mechanism. While this is primarily a means to identify potential victims and ensure they receive the right support, it is also a valuable source of information about current trafficking source countries and routes of entry.

88. Many law enforcement partners encounter trafficking activity, and some very successful anti-trafficking operations have been mounted on the basis of intelligence that originated at the front line of policing or immigration enforcement. However, some partners may not recognise the value of this information. Neighbourhood policing teams, for example, through their close relationships with communities and understanding of local issues will encounter unusual activity that may be a sign of trafficking activity. Police officers carrying out operations to tackle brothels may encounter trafficking victims and in the course of their investigations may find valuable intelligence about organised crime networks. We want to ensure staff can recognise this intelligence so we will explore ways to build this capacity, working with law enforcement agencies across the UK.

Seizing the Proceeds of Crime

89. We will attack the profits of the traffickers through greater use of asset recovery and financial investigation. We have formidable powers for investigating criminal finances and recovering assets from criminals which were introduced through the Proceeds of Crime Act 2002. This is an area where prosecutors play an important role in confiscating and seizing assets as well as forfeiture of property of traffickers.

90. However, only a small percentage of this is in relation to human trafficking, just 0.5% of recovered assets in the last financial year, leaving significant room for improvement. Previously, there was a perception that due to the international nature of trafficking, its profits were not available for recovery in the UK. More recent evidence, however, shows that this is not the case and that significant profit is generated within the UK, offering an opportunity to intervene even if the money is eventually intended for repatriation, notwithstanding the difficulties faced in enforcing recovery of assets. The forthcoming Organised Crime Strategy will set out our aim to improve the use of asset recovery and asset denial, taking a case by case approach against the most serious organised crime groups to determine the right approach.

91. The use of confiscation proceedings and asset recovery must be considered in every human trafficking related prosecution by the investigation and prosecution body. We will also explore the option of issuing clear guidance on when and how to initiate confiscation proceedings if we believe this is necessary.

92. To conduct a high-quality investigation there is a need to use financial investigation to develop intelligence, along with other techniques to prosecute and convict and pursue civil measures such as through the tax system and civil recovery. Building on the proposals in the forthcoming Organised Crime Strategy, further action is needed to step up this activity against traffickers. The UKHTC will continue to have access to a trained financial investigator, for deployment on specific human trafficking cases. We will further boost the capacity of this work in human trafficking investigations through better linking of Regional Asset Recovery Teams with human trafficking investigators.

93. By 31 December 2011 we will review whether the current legislation supports the effective prosecution of traffickers. Trafficking for labour exploitation is prosecuted under S. 4(2) of the Asylum & Immigration Act 2004, while trafficking for sexual exploitation is prosecuted under the Sexual Offences Act 2003. While there have been successful prosecutions under both,

there are some disparities which make the legislative framework less straightforward than it could be for prosecutors. In addition, the different levels of proof required mean that it is more difficult to prosecute for labour exploitation.

Tackling Demand

94. A key element in disrupting the market for trafficking and reducing its profitability is tackling demand by targeting those that pay for sexual services from trafficked women. There are a number of legislative measures which can assist law enforcement agencies in doing so. In particular the Policing and Crime Act 2009 amended the Sexual Offences Act 2003 to introduce an offence of paying for the sexual services of a prostitute subjected to force, deception, threats or any other form of coercion. This means that someone who pays for the sexual services of a trafficked woman (whether or not they know the woman has been trafficked) can be arrested and prosecuted. This offence came into effect on 1 April 2010. As of June 2011, the Crown Prosecution Service has identified that, since its enactment, 40 offences have been charged, which include cases of kerb crawling. Enforcement of this offence would target a key part of the chain that leads to women being trafficked into the country and help deter those that may consider paying for sexual services from someone who may be trafficked, thereby reducing the demand.

95. We must also tackle the demand for inexpensive, unprotected and often illegal labour. It is vital that we work to build an environment where this kind of labour is neither desired nor readily available. There is growing awareness among consumers of the harm caused by unethical business practices. But more needs to be done to increase understanding and encourage greater corporate moral and social responsibility within the private sector.

96. Other measures aimed at disrupting trafficking include closure orders, which allow the police to apply for a court order restricting access to premises associated with certain prostitution and pornography-related offences.

SECTION 7. CHILD VICTIMS OF HUMAN TRAFFICKING

97. Protection of child trafficking victims identified in the UK is paramount. We will therefore continue to work closely with partners to raise

awareness of child trafficking and ensure child victims are safeguarded and protected from re-trafficking.

We will update our core Government guidance on this issue, 'Safeguarding children who may have been trafficked' (2007) to ensure that practitioners are fully equipped with current information to better aid in the identification and safeguarding of victims. We will also identify opportunities to promote the child trafficking toolkit, developed by the London Safeguarding Children Board.

This will help enable early identification of trafficked children by local authorities and support quicker protection. We will also continue to work with the NSPCC in support of their Child Trafficking Advice and Information Line which provides valuable support and guidance to frontline agencies.

98. We will work with the police and the criminal justice system to ensure that trafficked children found to be involved in criminal activity are dealt rewith from a child safeguarding perspective and not unnecessarily criminalised. We will continue to work with the Association of Chief Police Officers and other law enforcement partners including CEOP, to raise awareness of recent guidance to the police on this issue. This will help ensure that, where trafficked children are found working in cannabis farms for example, police are trained to respond to these situations with a multi-agency safeguarding response involving local children's services. The CPS is involved in raising awareness of this issue and has recently updated guidance to prosecutors to provide greater direction and to lower the threshold for consideration of discontinuance for child suspects or victims.

99. We will continue to tackle the issue of trafficked children who go missing from local authority care in England and Wales. While there have been improvements in this area, the number of children who go missing is still too high. We will work with CEOP, who from 1 July 2011 have the lead for missing children, to ensure that the national capability supports this in the best way possible.

However, we know the greatest impact can be made through effective action to tackle this issue locally. We will build on the learning and experiences of partners in Hillingdon, Harrow, Hertfordshire and elsewhere to ensure that the safety of trafficked children is the first priority while they remain in local authority care and that the risks of them going missing or being rewith trafficked are minimised.

London Borough of Hillingdon's best practice in reducing numbers of missing children

Between 2007 and 2009, 79 young people in Hillingdon went missing from care shortly after arriving in the country. Many of these children were potential trafficking victims who had been brought into the country and Hillingdon established an operational model in partnership with law enforcement agencies with the aim of disrupting this issue. Hillingdon's response has three levels:

1) The Senior Local Safeguarding Children Board (LSCB) level is made up of senior managers working at the strategic level, from a range of agencies such as UK Border Agency, Police, Health and local authority.
2) The LSCB trafficking, exploitation and missing children subgroup is made up of middle managers. Its role focuses on policy, procedure and training. This group meets six to eight times a year; and includes representatives from CEOP, Police, UK Border Agency, as well as Local Authority teams and Non Governmental Organisations.
3) A multi-agency operational group made up of frontline staff meets every six weeks to discuss and assess the situation of every child reported missing in Hillingdon. This includes any children at risk of trafficking on arrival at the airport. This group uses and applies the trafficking toolkit to help identify trafficking issues, create child safeguarding plans, and arrange the de-briefing of victims.

This approach has significantly reduced the number of potentially trafficked children going missing in the local authority.

100. We will also ensure that the border represents a robust line of defence for child trafficking victims. Where children are being trafficked into the UK for exploitation they will be identified and safeguarded at the earliest possible opportunity.

101. Visa applications for children, particularly those travelling without parents, are subject to rigorous scrutiny. In addition to our normal process, if there are any concerns about the welfare of the child, a range of additional checks will be carried out. Unless we can be satisfied that the child will be

safe, their welfare will be protected, and that adequate arrangements have been made for their accommodation in the UK, we will not issue a visa.

102 UK Border Agency officers already maintain a high degree of vigilance in order to prevent human trafficking, particularly where this concerns children. We will continue to routinely question children and any accompanying adults to confirm there is no exploitative relationship. In cases where a further interview of either the child, or any other individual, is necessary, a specially trained UK Border Agency officer will undertake this. Leave to enter or remain will not be granted until the officer is satisfied with the arrangements made for the care and control of the child whilst in the UK and the intentions of the accompanying individual or sponsor confirmed.

103. Child trafficking needs a multi-agency response at high-risk entry points. Working with our partners we will therefore look to build on the success of the child safeguarding multi-agency teams such as Operations Paladin and Newbridge that are in place at some of our major ports to ensure there is appropriate level of coverage across the country, proportionate to the identified threat. We will ensure our intelligence supports these operations so that they can respond flexibly and ensure there are no 'safe routes' for those seeking to bring vulnerable young people into the UK.

Operation Newbridge is a joint approach to safeguard potentially trafficked children, involving children's services, the UK Border Agency and the police.

Its aim is to accept the safeguarding responsibility of children who may have been trafficked as soon as they land. The intention is to establish the circumstances, methodology and motivation for their arrival and journey to the UK, and in doing so prevent them from subsequently going missing.

Operation Paladin is a joint UK Border Agency and Metropolitan Police Service led operation. The team operates together to safeguard children arriving in the UK by identifying offenders and children at risk, investigating cases, gathering and sharing intelligence and working with other agencies.

104. Because of their vulnerability we will take additional steps to work with external partners to seek opportunities to raise awareness of the risks of child trafficking in source countries. The UK wants to send a strong message to traffickers that the UK will not tolerate any form of child abuse.

105. CEOP's International Child Protection Network (ICPN) is a key vehicle for awareness-raising work around child trafficking. For example, ICPN Regional Advisory Panels are active in Vietnam, Cambodia and Thailand (with one to follow in the Philippines). These Regional Advisory Panels bring together local law enforcement, NGOs, government agencies, industry and UK Government representation to coordinate awareness-raising measures and provide intelligence about the nature and scale of child exploitation in those countries.

CEOP's work in Vietnam

CEOP is continuing to build partnerships in source and transit countries to obtain more information on recruitment, trafficking routes, and methods. For example, CEOP recently conducted a scoping exercise of child trafficking issues within Vietnam and delivered training to professionals there so that they could educate children about the risks of trafficking.

106. In gathering intelligence on trafficking we will work to ensure the acute vulnerabilities of children are always taken into account. Where children are involved in de-briefing this activity will be delivered in a multi-agency framework with support and guidance from CEOP and the NSPCC's Child Trafficking Advice and Information Line where necessary.

107. Child trafficking victims are particularly vulnerable and the experiences they may have encountered are likely to have been traumatic. All agencies involved in supporting and protecting these vulnerable children will have their best interests at heart but it is critical that the processes used by agencies including local authorities, the police and UK Border Agency, contribute to a streamlined approach to gathering information on the child's needs and experiences. The Government is committed to minimising the impact on child victims and to ensuring that child victims are not unnecessarily asked to recount their experiences to different agencies. The NRM provides a valuable and useful tool for agencies to gather and share information on potential victims and, through work aimed at raising the awareness of the NRM, this strategy will help to ensure that agencies coordinate and share information to ensure the needs of child victims are appropriately assessed and met.

108. We recognise more needs to be done to stem the flow of human trafficking victims, particularly children, into the UK. That is why our

approach focuses on working with international partners to prevent vulnerable people from becoming trafficking victims in the first place. This, coupled with a strengthened border and better coordination of law enforcement activity, will help to minimise the potential for human trafficking victims to enter the UK. Where victims are brought to the UK we will ensure, through our improved victim care arrangements in England and Wales, that they have access to the support and care they need and deserve.

ANNEX A. HUMAN TRAFFICKING STRATEGY ACTIONS

Action	Paragraph	Action	Lead
Our response to combating human trafficking			
1	19	Work with the private sector to strengthen our overall approach to tackling trafficking.	Government
2	20	Explore what further role the public can play in identifying information about trafficking and how we can raise awareness and vigilance in particular communities.	Government
Improved victim identification and care			
3	26	Work with key partners both within the UK and the EU to implement the EU Directive on Human Trafficking effectively by April 2013.	Home Office
4	27	Raise the quality of decision-making under the NRM by running case review exercises and auditing decisions.	UKBA / SOCA
5	30	Raise awareness of trafficking among frontline staff through: Implementation of the findings of the trafficking and health project – to promote training and awareness of health professionals; and Working with the London Safeguarding Children Board to raise awareness amongst local authorities through their Child Trafficking Toolkit.	Home Office / UKBA / DoH / DfE
6	32	Continue to look for ways to enhance victim identification decision-making through driving up the quality of decisions and exploring the best match with immigration decision-making systems.	UKBA
7	37	Monitor delivery of victim care in conjunction with MOJ on a quarterly basis.	Home Office / MOJ

Annex A. (Continued)

Action	Paragraph	Action	Lead
Enhancing our ability to act early			
8	41	Explore greater opportunities to work with other countries – by focusing on targeting traffickers before they reach the UK and preventing more people from becoming victims in the first place.	Home Office / SOCA / UKBA/ FCO
9	43	Work with other agencies to ensure the information that we gather is as consistent and thorough as possible, and is fed consistently into our Organised Crime Mapping Tools.	SOCA
10	48	Focus on those transit and source countries from where the greatest threat originates, through the Country Business Plans.	Home Office / FCO
11	50	Through close working with FCO, engage foreign governments to ensure that common challenges are identified, and that they work with us to address those challenges.	Home Office / FCO
12	50 (box)	Work with other countries to ensure staff stationed in those countries have the tools necessary to lead the fight on trafficking.	Home Office / UKBA / FCO
13	53	Ensure de-briefing is set up in such a way that when one agency carries out a de-brief, they are gathering the information needed by all agencies – from recruitment, to transit route, to how they crossed the UK border, to activity within the UK.	SOCA / UKBA / Police
14	55	Work increasingly closely with the airline industry to enhance its knowledge of human trafficking and provide its staff with the tools needed to identify victims of trafficking and trigger an intervention.	UKBA
15	56	Continue to work with source countries to raise awareness among those who may be at risk of becoming a trafficking victim.	FCO / DfID
16	57	Continue to work with our FCC partners to identify best practice in deterring the use of people smugglers and, where possible, will work with our partners on coordinated education projects.	Government
17	60	Work closely with labour inspectorates across European Member States to achieve common standards on identifying and punishing labour exploitation.	Home Office / SOCA

Action	Paragraph	Action	Lead
18	61	Explore further the opportunities for establishing joint operations with overseas counterparts, building on the success of Operation Golf, a joint Metropolitan Police Service and Romanian National Police investigation team.	Home Office / Police
Smarter action at the Border			
19	67	Through the National Crime Agency and the Border Police Command, draw on the capability of a wide range of organisations and focus efforts on detection, intervention and the gathering and sharing of Intelligence.	Home Office NCA team / UKBA
20	67	Develop a set of UK specific risk indicators that can be deployed at our ports.	UKBA
21	70	Issue further guidance to all frontline border staff so that they understand what information is relevant to human trafficking, how it should be shared, and how to do this quickly so as to support effective intervention.	UKBA
22	72	Continue to deter and disrupt the use of false documentation and identities by working with airlines, strengthening checks on visa applicants, using appropriate biometric information, and working with overseas law enforcement and international partners to share information.	UKBA
23	73	Ensure our border staff have access to the right information and intelligence to identify and scrutinise those most at risk.	UKBA
24	74	Ensure that Intelligence gathered in country and overseas, including details held by the UKHTC on those convicted or suspected of trafficking, are passed to staff at the border.	SOCA / UKBA
Increasing coordination of our law enforcement efforts in the UK			
25	88	Work with law enforcement agencies across the UK to build capacity of police officers to recognise intelligence about organised crime networks.	Home Office
26	89	Attack the profits of the traffickers through greater use of asset recovery and financial investigation.	Home Office
27	91	Explore the option of issuing clear guidance on when and how to initiate confiscation proceedings, if we believe this is necessary.	Home Office

Annex A. (Continued)

Action	Paragraph	Action	Lead
28	92	Further boost the capacity of financial investigation in human trafficking investigations through better linking Regional Asset Recovery Teams (RARTs) with human trafficking investigators.	Police
29	93	By 31 December 2011 review whether the current legislation supports the effective prosecution of traffickers.	Home Office
Child Victims of Human Trafficking			
30	97	Identify opportunities to promote the child trafficking toolkit, developed by the London Safeguarding Children Board.	Home Office
31	97	Update core Government guidance – Safeguarding children who may have been trafficked.	DfE / Home Office
32	97	Continue to work with the NSPCC in support of their Child Trafficking Advice and Information Line (CTAIL).	Home Office
33	98	Work with the police and criminal justice partners to ensure that trafficked children found involved in criminal activity are safeguarded and not unnecessarily criminalised.	Home Office / CPS
34	99	Tackle the issue of trafficked children who go missing from Local Authority Care by working with CEOP, who from 1st July will have the lead for missing children, to ensure the national capability supports this in the best way possible.	Home Office / DFE / CEOP
35	103	Work with our partners and look to build on the success of the child safeguarding multi-agency teams such as Operation Paladin and Newbridge.	Police / Home Office / UKBA
36	104	Raise awareness in source countries of the risk of child trafficking.	Home Office / DfID / CEOP
37	106	Work to ensure the vulnerabilities of children are taken into account when debriefs take place.	Home Office / CEOP

End Notes

[1] United Nations Convention against Transnational Organised Crime

[2] Strategic Threat Assessment Child trafficking in the UK April 2010

[3] Project Acumen: Setting the Record: The trafficking of migrant women in the England and Wales off-street prostitution sector.

[4] Our best estimate of the numbers of trafficked children in the UK is based on the Child Exploitation and Online Protection Centre's Strategic Threat Assessment of child trafficking 2009 and 2010 which identified 325 and 287 potential child victims per annum respectively.

[5] Organised Crime Group Mapping

[6] UK Threat Assessment 09/10

[7] Home Office Research Report 15: 'Organised immigration crime: a post-conviction study'

INDEX

C

D

E

F

G

N

O

P

Q

R

S